TRANSFORMATIONS

TRANSFORMATIONS

Countertransference During
the Psychoanalytic Treatment of Incest,
Real and Imagined

Elaine V. Siegel

 THE ANALYTIC PRESS

1996   Hillsdale, NJ   London

Published by The Analytic Press, Inc.
Editorial Offices: 101 West Street, Hillsdale, NJ 07642

Typeset in Baskerville and Monet by Laserset, Inc., New York City

Library of Congress Cataloging-in-Publication Data

Siegel, Elaine V.
Transformations : countertransference during the psychoanalytic treatment of incest, real and imagined / Elaine V. Siegel.
   p.   cm.
 Includes bibliographical references and index.
 ISBN 0-88163-117-5
 1. Incest victims–Rehabilitation. 2. Countertransference
(Psychology). 3. Adult child sexual abuse victims–Rehabilitation.
I. Title.
RC560.I53S54   1996
616.85′8360651–dc20   95-12828
                                                           CIP

Printed in the United States of America
10 9 8 7 6 5 4 3 2 1

Sanity dissolving

Have you never stepped beyond
the intimate bonds of sanity?
Or seen the brittle world of two
dissolve like powder snow
Against the splintered fractions of an empty glass?
Or sensed, between the covers of sleep,
The hoarded fury of a wordless mass?
Once I closed a door
And felt it to the end.

A poem by Melanie,
who tore a hole into the sky

This book is for Eugene, Anita, Peter, Jeremy and Tamara, who will probably never read it.

Acknowledgments

I want to thank Paul E. Stepansky and Eleanor Starke Kobrin. They taught me how to "think" a book before writing it.

Contents

TRANSFORMATIONS

Chapter 1
Introduction

On Sunday, March 20, 1994, a TV film entitled "Ultimate Betrayal" was shown on WCBS. It purported to portray a true case of incest in which a father was convicted and forced to pay 2.3 million dollars for the damage he had inflicted on his daughter's life. There were horrendous scenes depicting a generally dysfunctional family, and then—nothing. No reflection. No comment. The condemned man never appeared. He was said never to have appeared at the trial either. Like him, the film makers and the station that broadcast the story of his breaking society's most sacrosanct taboo were silent. Viewers were left to draw their own conclusions. The message, if there was any, seemed to be: "Gee whiz, it really happened!" Nevertheless, the film was an acknowledgment that incest is not uncommon in our society. How to deal with it or what the motivation for it could be was not addressed. The film could also be viewed as the culmination and condensation of quite a few popular self-help books that offer clues to self-diagnosis and, of course, point the way to self-healing. Some of these books and articles go so far as to warn the reader that, even if no memory of incest or sexual abuse exists, it, like *The Shadow*, might still be lurking behind the lack of awareness if certain symptoms persist. The implication is, You may not know it, but You *were* sexually abused.

It is as though the current outpouring of and interest in tales about sexual abuse and incest, and how to deal with them, were filling up a hole. And, indeed, this hole in general acknowledgment of incestuous practices has long persisted, not because there are no warning signs, but because, in my opinion, the psychoanalytic community for too long has hidden behind the assumption that analysis of the fantasy elaborations caused by such trauma is more important than the fact of such trauma itself. These cases are analyzed in the privacy of the treatment situation; analysts are secure in the knowledge that they are following the dictates of their profession and of the father of the profession, Freud. That isolated cases might be the tip of an iceberg of widespread parental dysfunction has not seemed to be worth investigating in view of Freud's changing views. He at first thought parental seduction to be the cause of hysteria but modified his opinion considerably later on. (Freud, 1896). By 1914, however, Freud was able to say convincingly (and fruitfully for psychoanalysis) that "up to the present we have not succeeded in pointing to any difference in the consequences, whether fantasy or reality have the greater share in the events of childhood" (p. 370). He seems to have begun to doubt his reconstructions of his patients' histories and therefore abandoned seduction as the cause of hysteria.

It is noteworthy in this context that the label "seduction theory" was used by Ernest Jones and other historians of psychoanalysis. But Freud, speaking about the theme during the early period of his investigations, used stronger words, such as rape, abuse, attack, and trauma (Holland, 1989). But in 1932 Freud asserted, "I was driven to recognize in the end that these reports [of seduction] were untrue and so came to understand that hysterical symptoms are derived from fantasies and not from real occurrences" (p. 120). Clearly, he had abandoned the idea that incest causes hysteria, but not that incest could and did occur.

Psychoanalysts until the 1970s appear to have taken each case of incest as a solitary happening that could be analyzed but only, we find out in retrospect, with difficulty. Other troubled people who seemed to show telltale signs of what might or might not have been incest were deemed unanalyzable and received other forms of treatment. Even though some material has been forthcoming lately, the dearth of solid psychoanalytically informed case material from which inferences for further research can be drawn is amazing in view of the fact that my own informal survey of 40 colleagues elicited the information that they had all dealt with cases of incest or sex abuse in their long time practices.

Simon (1992) goes so far as to accuse the psychoanalytic community of defensively knowing, and at the same time not knowing, about actual incest and the trauma inflicted by adults on children (p. 962). He sees the psychoanalytic community as sharing the same adaptively defensive oscillations of disavowal and denial as do the victims of incest. In a scholarly survey, he clearly delineates the inconsistencies in psychoanalytic theory and the problems psychoanalytic technique must overcome in the treatment of people who have suffered incest. One of the main issues, according to Simon, is the unclear conceptualization of what the term incest refers to and how this term relates to "seduction and trauma." Simon feels that many psychoanalysts now subscribe to the opinions stated by the 1988 panel of the American Psychoanalytic Association "On the Seduction Hypothesis." The panel held that the existence of incest and its potentially devastating role has always been known but that its prevalence and importance have been vastly underrated. I myself understand incest to be the unwanted and unwarranted bodily manipulation of a child by a parent, grandparent, or older sibling for purposes of satisfying the sexual needs of the aggressor.

It is interesting that the rather official statements by psychoanalysts about their position vis-à-vis seduction and trauma were made *after* Masson's 1984 battering ram of a book shattered complacency in many quarters. As is well known, Masson falls prey to a few lapses of logic himself. He accuses Freud of abandoning his seduction theory in a self-serving way. But what Freud (1896) actually abandoned was his previous assumption that there was a causal connection between the specific aetiology of hysteria and passive sexual experience before puberty. Until the end of his life, however, he stressed the pathogenic effect of childhood seduction and sexual overstimulation (Freud, 1917, 1918, 1933).

Despite his misrepresentations, Masson did lead the psychoanalytic community into reexamining its position vis-à-vis the actual occurrence of incest. There are now regular workshops on the topic of incest sponsored by the American Psychoanalytic Association. Case reports are surfacing, and there are serious studies under way to examine the effects of incest, technical considerations during treatment, and so on (Spruiell, 1986; Weinshell, 1986, 1988; Herman and Schatzow, 1987; Diamond, 1989; Shengold, 1989; Levine, 1990). Most important, Weil's (1989) contribution goes a long way to clearing up some confusions. He studied 100 clinical cases and investigated in depth the symptoms and dreams of children who had been exposed to erotic contact with, to physical punishment by, adults, or both.

Even so, agreement has not been reached on such crucial issues as what is, and what is not, incest. After all, Freud analyzed his own daughter, which could certainly be viewed as symbolic incest. Lipton (1977) has an intriguing view of such happenings as analysts' analyzing their own children: according to him, Freud considering the unobjectionable positive transference outside technique, took it for granted. He therefore saw no need to include it in his papers on technique. Because he made the distinction between analytic and nonanalytic relationships, Freud was able to analyze his daughter without experiencing any contradictions. The knowledge that psychoanalysis influences the analysand's entire life does not seem to have entered his decision to analyze his daughter. Apparently, he felt that the analytic hour was confined to its temporal space and thus would not interfere with his paternal relationship with his daughter. But can the symbolic incest in such action be denied? I hope that the practice has disappeared. To my knowledge, no published accounts of present day parent–child analysis exist.

Still, in the unconscious or even the consciousness of every psychoanalytic clinician, there is the knowledge that Freud made an exception to his own rules when analyzing his daughter. The need persists to view this act either as unobjectionable—after all, Anna Freud was undeniably one of the greatest contributors to psychoanalysis—or as symbolically incestuous. If Freud's analysis of his own daughter was symbolically incestuous, was it damaging? Perhaps, in view of Anna Freud's lasting contribution, not very damaging. Or was it?

How analysts deal with this event has, in my opinion, much to do with the inevitable transference to Freud himself. Despite the disavowal of many, I do not believe that one can become a psychoanalyst without coming to terms with the "Father of Psychoanalysis." The transferences of the many eventually become the stated attitude of the community as a whole. Like all transferences, they shift and are subject to influences from society. Even if unacknowledged, they continue to exert their influence. This much is self-evident. Yet despite theoretical knowledge about Freud and his work, the ever-present transference to Freud in many psychoanalysts may have stymied some creative treatment innovations or investigations that could have

led to more psychoanalytically acceptable formulations, especially in such troubling areas as the treatment of incest and
sexual abuse of children.

The unresolved transference to Freud as fountainhead of all
psychoanalytic wisdom has grave consequences for the experience and use of countertransference as well. I know from my
own experience and from the supervision of young colleagues
that it is necessary to come to terms with one's oedipal wishes
toward Freud-the-Father before one can experience, in all its
magnificent—and sometimes horrific—aspects, resonances of
the ubiquitous countertransference. My understanding of
countertransference includes reactivation of various compo-
nents of coanesthetic perception in the analyst which can be
used in conjunction with the patient's productions as bridges
to verbal interpretation. I have called these regressive phenomena somatic countertransference (Siegel, 1988, p. 211). Because
my countertransference, especially my somatic responses, was
so often a valuable guide in the treatment of those patients
who convinced me that they had experienced incest, I will take
the plunge and talk about it as it unfolded in each case. I feel
free to do so because I no longer practice and am therefore
less constrained by how my publications might impinge on
future and present analysands. Everyone whose tale is written
here has concluded his or her interaction with me.

I am intentionally using this phraseology because at times
the transferences of incest victims took on a "real" as opposed
to an "as if" quality. It has been felt by some classic psychoanalysts (Deutsch, 1942; Greenson, 1968) that awareness of this
"as if" quality of the transference is precisely what makes certain patients analyzable. This, in my opinion, is true only when
the analyst responds as the real, as opposed to the analytic,
object. Without a doubt, patients build real inner object representations of their analysts that prove to be beneficial in the
long run. But these object representations are based on the
psychic reality of the patient, not on the "real," that is the
nonanalytic, attributes of the analyst. Therefore, I find it
entirely unobjectionable when an analysand temporarily needs
to see me as a real mother, father, or lover, as long as I do not
abandon my interpretive mode. I make this rather obvious statement because it has to do with the way I handled my
countertransferences. Although in this book I will talk more
or less freely about what I felt and how these feelings became

useful, I will strip certain identifiable aspects from my patients' histories to protect their privacy. Nevertheless, I have given the people about whom I am reporting fictitious names that in some ways remind me of them so as to give more immediacy to my clinical descriptions. After all, I never called anyone Mrs. A or Mr. X!

Some particularly instructive cases had to be omitted because the patients may have found it objectionable to reveal themselves even in a disguised manner; not that I discussed in detail what I wanted to write, but occasionally they would remark, "Nobody should know this," or the like. I did not approach those patients for permission. Still, their remarks had left an impression on me or found their way into my copious notebooks along with the remarks of the patients reported herein. In what I now see as a countertransferential response, I found it necessary to write down as many details as I could remember of many analyses, primarily because I was then so touched and often confused by what I was told. I think I must have been afraid to lose the contents of what my patients told me or even lose the memory of the patients themselves if I did not in some way make them unforgettable.

I now recognize this strategy of writing as my reaction to the fate of my family during and after the second world war. Perhaps my strenuous countertransference efforts on behalf of my patients-as-symbolic-family were also motivated by an attempt to save myself from the guilt of living in the U.S.A., away from my family. And I wonder still more about my seemingly unanalyzable compulsion to record sessions. There were, of course, secondary gains. Supervisors and senior colleagues liked my thoroughness, or what passed for it. Patients often responded with pleasure when I seemed to remember details that they deemed unimportant or that helped them to untangle complicated connections. Note taking and remembering in time became good tools. I made my notes during the breaks between sessions, only on rare occasions jotting a word or two to myself during sessions.

A WORD ABOUT COUNTERTRANSFERENCE AS I USE IT

I wrote about the occurrence and use of somatic countertransference when I reported on my work with homosexual women (Siegel, 1988). I spoke of it again three years later, when I wrote about the many treatments of children I had conducted prior and concomitant to becoming a psychoanalyst (Siegel, 1991). In this book I examine further when, how, and why I chose to use countertransference as information and guide to the inner happenings of my analysands and psychoanalytic psychotherapy patients who had suffered incest.

Let me restate in greater detail what I mean by "countertransference." Although the controversy of what is and what is not countertransference has not really been resolved, "demonstrating one's awareness of countertransference has, in Abend's (1989) words, become an almost obligatory aspect of presenting one's professional bona fides, regardless of one's theoretical preference" (p. 392). I don't see the situation as quite so heavily charged with differing attitudes toward countertransference. After all, analysts have to come to terms with their preferences about when and how to use countertransference, and these preferences often dictate which analytic school one tends to follow. As long as one does not become messianic about one's theoretical position and tries to deal with one's own reactivated conflicts while keeping analysands' interests in mind, all approaches, in my view, produce acceptable results. Controversy keeps psychoanalysts on their theoretical toes, so to speak, and makes them examine and reexamine how they affect the analyses they conduct.

Abend goes on to warn of the pitfalls inherent in the current, more accepting attitude toward countertransference. For instance, underlying the debunking of the older notion of countertransference as a hindrance to the ability to analyze, one may find value judgments, such as those surrounding authority issues. Abend also points out that certain countertransference attitudes might influence an analyst's technique in providing a more intentionally supportive, nurturing, or holding emotional climate for some or all analysands (p. 391). While these remarks may appeal to adherents of certain schools of psychoanalytic thought, they can also be read as an acknowledgment that not all psychoanalysts always stay neutral or are above manipulating the analytic environment. For myself, in 1988 I formulated what I still believe today: that the feelings induced in me by my patients' transferences represent a possible source of the reactivation of my past conflicts and a way to deal further with my own pathological defenses. More important, I view these feelings as indicators (not as proof!) of what might be going on in the patient at that time (Siegel, 1988, p. 196).

The uses of countertransference or its avoidance are often linked to the concept of neutrality. Is the analyst overinvolved when being empathic or acknowledging therapeutic intent? I was delighted to come on a formulation by Levy and Inderbitzin (1992) that deals concisely and thoughtfully with this issue. They state

> We define psychoanalytic neutrality as both a listening and an interpretive stance that encourages the emergence of as many of the multiple determinants of mental conflicts as are discoverable via the psychoanalytic method. It is the inevitability of the presence of this multitude of factors and the analyst's openness to and pursuit of the fullest possible understanding of them during interpretive work that constitute neutrality in relation to interpretation, not an indifference to the outcome of the convergence of these multiple factors . . . . the interpretive process remains neutral to the extent it explores as many of the determinants of mental conflict as possible. Interventions that interfere with the discovery or elucidation of further material related to a particular conflict are no longer neutral [pp. 996–997].

I wish I could have been this direct in my own thinking about such matters when I struggled to be clear in my understanding of how I could be neutral while experiencing strong countertransferential feelings. Levy and Inderbitzin outline a position with which I firmly concur: it is how one uses one's interpretive skills that determines neutrality.

It is beyond the scope of these introductory remarks for me to examine the many other excellent contributions to the understanding of neutrality, empathy and therapeutic intent. Let me emphasize that here, too, one encounters countertransferential issues that surface for every psychoanalyst and must be resolved according to personal analytic experience, training, and style. We all know that the traditional concept of abstinence, which is so closely linked with neutrality, has come to mean something else since Freud (1915) decreed that "analytic technique requires of the physician that he should deny to the patient who is craving for love the satisfaction she demands. The treatment must be carried out in abstinence" (p. 165). This is not a description of neutrality. It is singularly "unneutral" in its emphasis that something—abstinence—must be adhered to. This does not mean that I disagree with the underlying premise. I merely wish to point to inconsistencies in our most cherished treatment traditions, which, in turn, influence one's analytic instrument, including countertransference. Abstinence, by the way, is no longer deemed applicable to both partners in the analytic dyad. Freud (1915) thought that the patient, too, should refrain from drive gratification while the analyst stayed away from transference gratifications. By now, it is only the analyst who, to the best of his or her ability, abstains.

Even given all these important aspects, it was still awareness of my countertransference that kept me analytically productive while treating patients who had experienced incest. Foremost in my continuous exploration of countertransference, and before I could use appropriately what I discerned, was an examination of what I felt about Freud and his work. My awe and envy of his brilliance, my despair of never being able to emulate him or to climb even half way up his tower of excellence stunted my use of countertransference for a long time. The phallic nature of my associations perturbed me until I recognized them as part of an identification with an aggressor who was in my imagination, Freud. Nevertheless, as I fought with feeling myself alternately to be a thief of Freud's insights and his obedient child, a Freud killer and a Freud expander, I gradually came to use my own analytic instrument with greater assurance and with greater success. It seemed to me that I struggled with my oedipal rivalry with Freud at the same time that my patients engaged in their particular transferential repetitions. As my confusions cleared, so did theirs. Throughout, I maintained an attitude of not sharing my feelings with analysands, though I was not always as successful in this as I might have wished. I discovered that my analysands' internal receivers were much more finely tuned than mine; they generally knew what I was feeling anyway. Little (1951) surely was on the right track in observing that

> unconsciously we tend to identify [also] with the patient's superego and id, and thereby with him, in any prohibition on getting well, and in his wish to stay ill and dependent, and by doing so we may slow down his recovery. Unconsciously we may exploit a patient's illness for our own purposes, both libidinal and aggressive, and *he will quickly respond to this* [p. 34, italics added].

As my analysands wrestled with the distortions and destructions of their childhoods, they became hypervigilant to any real or transferential signal that I might be yet another abuser or distorter of facts. Simultaneously, the repetition compulsion drove me to silently and in fantasy to replay my personal oedipal drama in relationship to an imagined professional parent, Freud. This was true particularly when I treated patients who later turned out to have suffered incest; in these cases, my own drama could shield me from the full impact of the transgressions that had happened in my analysands' lives. When I recognized a certain facet of my own past as relevant, the defensive obfuscation and obsession with Freud and theory ceased while my countertransferential responses became more reliable. I will enlarge on my personal evolution later.

DISTINGUISHING INCEST FROM OTHER TRAUMATA

Is it possible that many of my colleagues have walked similar defensive paths? Surely it must be so. Otherwise, how could so many psychoanalysts have accepted unquestioningly Freud's insight in a letter to Fliess that "there are no indications of reality in the unconscious, so that one cannot distinguish between truth and fiction that has been cathected with affect (Accordingly, there would remain the solution that the sexual fantasy invariably seizes on the theme of the parents.)" (Masson, 1985, p. 264).

While this sweeping generalization is as true today as it was almost 100 years ago, there are now additional insights based on clinical experience that allow us to formulate more fully—if not always with 100% success—who was sexually or incestuously abused. There are still no entirely reliable statistics available. Estimates of incestuous or abusive sexual experiences in childhood range from 25% for girls and 10% for boys (Herman, Russel, and Trackl, 1986; Herman and Schatzow, 1987). Father–daughter incest appears to be more common than mother–son incest. Only very few cases are known of mother–daughter or father–son incest (Wolf and Alpert, 1991). Seventy-five to eighty percent of abused girls identified their father or stepfather as the one "who did it " (Irving, 1964).

We know from the psychiatric, epidemiologic, and social work literature what the pathological effects and family characteristics surrounding incest and sexual abuse are (Woodbury and Schwartz, 1971; Finkelhor, 1979; Goodwin, McCarthy, and

DiVasto, 1981; Mrazek and Kempe, 1981; Westen et al., 1990). In addition, Shengold (1991) feels "that in cases of massive dissociative defense and of denial, a traumatic childhood should be suspected—but not assumed" (p. 56). Armed with this information, psychotherapists and psychoanalysts, can, once the psychoanalytic process unfolds, usually venture an informed, always cautious opinion about which of their patients has actually been molested. It goes without saying that such an undertaking is fraught with danger and can smack of therapist omnipotence. Still, patience on both sides of the therapeutic dyad usually lets the tale emerge with enough certainty to allow the patient renewed growth.

Relatively little of the literature actually presents case material. Particularly informative psychoanalytic reports are to be found in the collection by Levine (1990) and a 1992 "Symposium on Survivors of Child Sexual Abuse" in the journal *Psychoanalytic Dialogues* (Symposium, 1992). I will return to these contributions when I focus on how theory informed the treatments I conducted. I was challenged by some of the formulations offered. My past clinical experience did not always validate newer theoretical formulations such as those of Davies and Frawley (1992). Further, it is impossible to ignore the poignant work of Shengold (1989), who has dealt for many years with a subject others are silent about, and the wealth of information in Kramer and Akhtar's (1991) contribution. Most of the patients I discuss here were similar to Shengold's population: interrupted in crucial areas of development but possessing of character and ego strengths that helped them adapt to and deal with their untenable familial situations.

This book is informed by the hope that my case histories will help to clarify certain issues about the analytic treatment of patients who have undergone childhood sexual trauma. In particular, I wish to describe the analysis and psychoanalytic psychotherapy of one type of sexual trauma, namely, incest that occurred in childhood. I have found that the symbolic incest or abuse of children by persons outside of their families produced different, though similar, symptoms. All the patients about whom I am reporting here had deeply repressed any memory of having been incestuously used. Therefore, they differed from the group who claim to remember their abuse. As a matter of fact, I include two case histories of analysands who thought they had been grievously used in an incestuous manner but later retracted this claim. I have also found that the act of maternal incest (Kramer, 1983) caused psychic damage different from that of father–daughter incest. Although the literature stresses the prevalence of father–daughter incest, I can report on only two such events here and have analyzed only one additional case of father–daughter incest.

I have reported elsewhere three cases of children who were incestuously or sexually abused (Siegel, 1991). Here my focus is on adults. Sherkov's (1990a, b) solid work was not yet available when I treated the children. In the cases of the children, it was important to pay attention to their disjointed, hyper-cathected and only partially symbolic motility and playing. This was not true of the adults I treated, although some literally bounced around on the couch or in other ways spoke on and off the couch through the language of their movements. My adult analysands functioned relatively well but were unhappy and often depressed. Some resorted to forms of body language, somatic complaints, and enactments on the couch to let me know what they felt. At the beginning of treatment none suspected being victims of incest. I believe that people who have conscious knowledge of such happenings have suffered a fate different from that of those who don't remember. If the event took place in the past, repression failed to protect them. Their inner structures therefore must be different from my analysands and psychotherapy patients. Another common feature among my group was their disbelief once the trauma had been uncovered.

Beyond these two features I venture no generalizations about these patients. As a matter of fact, I strenuously object to the attempt, no matter how well meaning, to categorize people who have experienced incest as a separate diagnostic category. Levine (1990) similarly states that "accumulated data do not seem to support the definition of a specific syndrome that is unique to this group of patients" (p. 197). It follows that I do not agree with the conclusion of Marcus (1989) that incest is a prototype for boundary disturbances in borderline personality organization (p. 203), though in some people it might be the causal agent. I have found ample borderline organizations and diffusion in patients who did not experience incest to refute that statement.

I have similar reservations about the work of Davies and Frawley (1992). In the "Symposium on Survivors of Childhood Sexual Abuse" they report that it is necessary to recognize "the simultaneous coexistence and alternation of multiple (at least two) levels of ego organization" (p. 5). Around this and other perceptions they formulate a profile that makes their incest survivors recognizable. They also felt that they had to "enter, rather than interpreting, the dissociated world of the abused child" (p. 30). They seem to have taken this plan of therapeutic action quite literally and moved beyond the usual trial identifications. Above all, they seem to have concretized their concept of the "child in the adult." They describe that "on one level we hear the cries of the terrified, abused child recoiling from the presence of her seducer" (p. 29) when they undertake to interpret the transferential avoidance of the therapist's closeness. The other level is the patient as "demanding, insatiable, and constantly critical abuser" (p. 29). In all, it seems the authors are intent on describing a subgroup of patients. I prefer the stance of Gabbard and Twemlow (1994), who cautiously suggest that mother–son incest might, under certain conditions, lead to the formation of a "hypervigilant, narcissistic character pathology" (p. 174). With equal caution, they suggest that even such severely traumatized patients might be amenable to psychoanalysis (p. 187).

In the case reports to follow I believe that in the majority of cases the psychoanalytic stance of listening, interpreting the transference, including genetic antecedents and then working through, brought about desired results. I did not find it necessary to construct special parameters that were generally applicable. On occasion, I had to allow for additional contact by telephone or comply with a patient's wish to sit up and look at me. These infrequent happenings could invariably be analyzed. As a matter of fact, although I recognize the investigations by Davies and Frawley and Marcus as useful attempts to add to the by now proverbial widening scope of psychoanalysis, my clinical experience informs me that it is not only increased knowledge about developmental levels and more accurate diagnostic skills that lead to favorable treatment results. The all-important complement to those clinical tools is the deepened awareness of psychoanalytic clinicians to their particular analytic instruments. If we paid as much attention to research about the evolution and development of our most important psychoanalytic tool, namely, our ability to resonate, we might find that psychoanalysis is more widely applicable than we now deem possible.

This admonition to continue one's self-analysis may be a time-worn one, but I think it needs reinforcement. Generally, each patient elicits resonances specific to his or her treatment situation, though, of course, analysts learn to listen within the confines of their particular receiving instrument and can comment meaningfully on their style and mode of being with individual patients. Nevertheless, I have found continuing and often painful self-analysis the most reliable and useful treatment tool. Perhaps because I continued to scrutinize myself along with my incestuously used patients, I experienced them as adults who had learned the hard way to take care of themselves and who did not need more than my emotional and interpretive presence to resolve their dilemmas. In fantasy we have all experienced incest. Why, then, assume that people who have actually lived through it are weaker, or less able to use interpretation, than we are? It might take them a bit longer to trust enough, but in essence they listen and work through, use interpretation and insight just as the rest of us do, namely, in a distorted way. To recognize and interpret the distortions remains the therapeutic task, not the naming of yet another syndrome, diagnosis, or specific grouping.

For the same reason I object to the title "survivor" for the particular group of analysands I describe here. At best the word imparts a flavor of the melodramatic; at worst it underscores the existing sadomasochistic fixations in many, but not all, of these patients. After all, except for one case, I am not talking about battered or otherwise physically attacked people. I have no real experience with such cruelly misused people. Their psychic structure must of necessity differ from that of the groups mentioned. For the most part, my analysands not only were misused by their parents, but were also loved by them, albeit in a self-serving, primitive, and unempathic way. I do not wish to make excuses for the inexcusable, nor do I wish to imply that my analysands, as children, were, unduly seductive, a point of view that seems to have been the fashion in earlier times (Irving, 1964; Furst, 1967). I do want to point out that trying to understand these manipulators and abusers of chil-

dren might be the best way eventually to eliminate such practices by preventing them. But that is a subject for another book.

A BRIEF LISTING OF THE RELEVANT LITERATURE

I will confine myself to important case reports. Much of what
is now available was not yet in print when I worked with my
analysands. I often struggled in the dark but was buoyed by
the publications of major clinicians whose impact on my work
I will discuss in more detail later (Ferenczi, 1930, 1949; Kohut,
1959, 1971; Shengold, 1963; Greenacre, 1971; Rascovsky and
Rascovsky, 1972).

The majority of the reports I cite are about daughters who
were incestuously abused by their fathers. One review (Wolf
and Alpert, 1991), in analyzing the material collected, states
that "for about half the cases, abuse of girls began in early
childhood; it seldom began in adolescence" (p. 311). This finding is consistent with my own.

Several papers explore in an illuminating way single cases
of incestuously misused daughters (Ehrenberg, 1987; Bernstein,
1989, 1990; Dewald, 1989; Marcus, 1989; Huizenga, 1990;
Lisman-Piesczanski, 1990; King and Dorpat, 1992). Reports
about several cases, mainly in the form of clinical vignettes or
highlights of treatments, allow for examination of similarities
and differences of psychic wounds suffered. In studying them,
however, I became convinced that none of the authors had
sufficient material to generalize for the whole population of
girls and women who had experienced incest in childhood
(Shengold, 1963; Katan, 1973; Berry, 1975; Kramer, 1983; Soll,
1984–1985; Cohler, 1987; Nachmani, 1987; Bernstein, 1989,
1990; Raphling, 1990; Siegel, 1991). Almost all the authors
talk about the primitive defenses used. Disassociation, repression, and the repetition compulsion are mentioned again and
again. I cautiously agree that this constellation of defense
mechanisms does occur in this population, but this fact alone
does not make the inner lives of these women very different
from those of others I have analyzed.

There are fewer case reports of males having been incestuously misused by their mothers (Margolis, 1977; Silber, 1979;
Shengold, 1989; Gabbard and Twemlow, 1994). It is not at all

clear whether this dearth of published material reflects actual occurrence or whether such abused boys and men do not come for treatment. Perhaps males in our society are trained to deny that they might have been victimized. Although Margolis (1977) and Shengold (1980) speak of the heightened sense of specialness and fantasized entitlement in males sexually abused by their mothers, Shengold goes on to say that his patient "was saved from homosexuality or at least some grave deformation of his sexual life" (p. 473) by the incest with his mother. The analysis of two sons who were incestuously used by their mothers has taught me otherwise. Homosexuality appeared like a desirable but unobtainable goal to these young men until they could loosen the grasp of the devouring aspect of the internalized mother.

There appears to be agreement among many that mothers who abuse their sons and daughters incestuously are themselves more psychologically impaired than are fathers who commit the same acts. I am not at all certain that I agree. The inner constellation that allows incest to occur may look different in males and in females, but the lack of repression, the ability to indulge oneself at the cost of another, and manipulation of helpless and weaker individuals is not gender specific. Fathers who commit incest are as unwilling to let their daughters individuate as are mothers who take their sexual satisfaction with their sons (Margolis, 1977; Kramer, 1990; Gabbard and Twemlow, 1994). This became clear to me when I treated a case of father–son incest (Siegel, 1991). The patient in that case, however, was not an adult but a child whose immature ego development was further retarded by his father's sexual demands on him. In my opinion, it is the inner and outer circumstances of particular cases that permit comparative judgments about the degree of impairment of different perpetrators. And the depth of damage they inflict on their hapless offspring does not necessarily correlate with the amount of inner destruction sustained by incestuous parents themselves. On the basis of my clinical experience, I have concluded that deeply disturbed parents do not always cause the greatest damage. In some ways, by their behavior and affect, they convey to their abused children that what they have done together is not right. Thus, the reality perception and sense of self of some children of psychotics do not become as vague as when parents who function more appropriately in a social sense try to instill a sense of guilt and shame or threaten punishment if the child complains. Double binds and sudden reversals of affect, as well as self-protective denial when confronted by the outside world, produce much more anxiety than does the open admission of a shared wrong. Reviewing all the cases I report on in this book, I find that I cannot assign mothers more pathology than fathers.

REFLECTIONS ON THE UNFOLDING OF COUNTERTRANSFERENCE IN THE TREATMENT OF THE AFTERMATH OF INCEST

In the years before the second world war, my family occasionally spent summers on the farm of a great-uncle in Silesia, then part of Eastern Germany. The prosperous village, surrounded by wheat fields and well-tended forests, was characterized by special pride in the appearance of the farm houses. Housewives prided themselves on their flower beds and lace curtains. Not so a low, thatched cottage somewhat outside the village. Mud spattered, its small windows blind with dirt, it seemed overrun by children. Then an active and curious preschooler, I wanted to play with the children but was halted in my getting-acquainted foray toward the cottage by one of the women who worked on the farm. "They eat cats and dogs," she warned me, pointing to the children. When I asked why, she told me that "they didn't know any better."

At the dinner table that night, I asked why we didn't teach the people in the cottage to eat beef and chicken like we did. It seemed to me we had plenty to go around. The silence that followed my question startled me. Finally, out of the silence, my great-uncle turned toward me and said: "You must never go near them. They mate with each other." I had absolutely no idea what "mate with each other" meant, but I clearly perceived something else: everyone around the table was afraid and made me afraid. My heart pounded. I had difficulty breathing. My stomach felt constricted as though I had done a forbidden thing. Despite my certainty that I had done nothing wrong, I felt guilty for, somehow, by my question, having trespassed on an adult secret domain I had no right to share. In addition, I was made uncomfortable by observing some of the facial expressions around me. My great-aunt and uncle had turned pale and grave; my mother stared straight ahead as she did when I was naughty; the farm workers either smirked, blushed, or turned pale like their employer. I felt like saying, "But I don't eat cats and dogs."

During the treatment of people who had "mated" with a forbidden partner, I often recalled this scene. I had never really forgotten it, but merely suppressed it as unimportant until, during my own analysis, I rediscovered its relevance as part of my sensitivity to the language of the body and as a possible screen memory. It was precisely this sensitivity that tuned my analytic responsiveness. Each time an analysand came close to revealing his or her terrible secret, I had the same response I had experienced when, as a child, I asked about the people in the cottage. It did not occur when I treated two people who thought they had been incestuously used by their parents but later recanted.

I began to feel like Cassandra prophesying doom when a patient, usually after much preceding work, would bring me a dream or an association that elicited the multifaceted bodily response I've just described. When, for the third or fourth time, I forecast (to myself and my notebook only) incest as the next memory of a patient, I began seriously to question my technique. Was I unconsciously revealing, suggesting, or pushing into the patient my own fantasies? I sought supervision and was helped to view myself in a different light, in which it was difficult for me to be any different from my colleagues in demonstrating predictive ability or to question the opinion that the analysis of fantasy elaboration of incestuous trauma was more important than the trauma itself. I just wanted to be a good psychoanalyst, rational, objective, and neutral; never mind this sensibility. Much later, in 1988, Dorpat asserted:

> The ability to understand and to interpret nonverbal communication distinguishes (in my opinion) superior psychoanalysts and therapists from those who perform less competently. Undeveloped capacities for decoding nonverbal communication render analysts opaque to a rich source of affective communication. In using one's countertransference as a listening instrument, one should listen with one's total self, including one's somatic reactions (p. xvi).

Given my struggles with my transference to Freud, I would have cringed had I read something like that during those early years.

I then believed that such primary-process related phenomena as the ability to understand body language bore the stamp of pathology—in myself and others. In an utterly ego-dystonic kind of way, I saw myself forced to side with Ferenczi (1930), who convinced himself that patients must fully relive their traumatic past in order to benefit maximally from analytic treatment. The volatility and drivenness in several of my patients who were plagued by the aftereffects of their incestuous trauma seemed to me then to prove that reliving the trauma was, in such instances, unavoidable. Yet I was equally clear in my understanding that no adult can ever completely recapture the actual experiences of the distant past. We must be content with the mere emanations of the past.

But what if the past is powerfully present? I decided then, and still believe, now, that Ferenczi was on the right track in believing that patients must be given the space to experience to the fullest, whatever the repetition compulsion brings to light. What I could not reconcile with my own clinical experiences was the way he appeared to steer patients toward lack of control. I found over and over again that staying emotionally available, yet restrained in my responsiveness, set the stage for remembering, so that a verbal bridge could be found for the seemingly inchoate emotional waves that washed over both my patients and me. The struggle for insight was indeed like the struggle for oxygen when a wave breaks over one's head. I could best cope with this wave by staying calm on the outside even when seething with outrage and reawakened responses to my own past, or when suffocating under the dead weight of curtailed associations, the patients' affective absence, or prolonged stalemates during which I could not find my way through the maze of vague remembrances, transference enactments on the couch and off, and my responses to them. And my patients seemed to read at least partially what I felt and often tried unconsciously to manipulate me into abandoning my interpretive work.

To return to Ferenczi, I thought his clinical experiences were probably close to mine, but I had misgivings about his handling of those experiences. Valenstein (1962) remarked that "Ferenczi's emphasis was really on repeating and experiencing rather than remembering and understanding" (p. 320). As a result of such pondering, I put myself into a double bind analogous to what my patients often experienced with their parents. On one hand, I was certain that my analysands' oscillations between emotional outbursts, blind reliving, and distancing from me were absolutely essential for them. On the other hand, I could not subscribe to the way in which Ferenczi seemed to embrace and even encourage these happenings. Finally, I realized that both blind, emotive reliving and reliving tamed by insight are necessary for inner changes to take place: repetition that is affectively meaningful and leads, by way of genetic interpretation and reconstruction, to insight, and, if the patient needs to do so, reliving in the transference what was so hideous in the past. This means that the analyst is sometimes seen as a symbolic abuser.

My own ruminating associations and agonized scrutiny of theory and technique finally led me to understand that the intellectual games I played with myself had to do with warding off the knowledge that analysands for whom I was doing my best were nevertheless experiencing me at times as their abusers. I was able to admit this to myself only after understanding that one way in which I had coped with my Silesian memory was by identifying with the superego figures contained therein, namely, my great-aunt and great-uncle. As long as I stood with them, nobody could accuse me of eating cats and dogs or of mating with the disguised grandparental couple. With this insight, it became easier to handle my physical discomfort when I had to deal with myself in my patients' transferences as the abusing brute. Like my great-uncle, I allowed myself the affect—repugnance, even horror—when confronted by incest, but I also accepted these feelings as approximate; that is, I temporarily permitted myself to be censorious rather than neutral. I was able to cope with being seen as unempathic and brutal. The societal need for the incest barrier to remain intact also came into focus and helped me to empathize further with patients who were forced by life events to stand outside of the norm.

My conflict in accepting the transferential role of the abuser calls to mind the work of Rascovsky and Rascovsky (1972), who remind us that filicide preceded parricide. After all, Oedipus was mutilated and left to die as an infant, abandoned by the very woman he was to make his wife after killing her husband, his father. I am still filled with awe and experience a mild echo of my Silesian vignette when I recall the treatments that revealed incest and an aftermath invariably marked by both parricidal and filicidal tendencies, as though Oedipus had not yet met his punishment or were still wandering the earth in eternal despair.

When the incest barrier fails, the emotional volcano against which it was erected once again erupts. The child's developing ego is swept up by the parental excess; becomes split between love and fear, guilt, and shame, and finally needs to build formidable barriers against remembering. Psychoanalysts, too, erect barriers. They find words to express the inexpressible so as to facilitate change and, perhaps also, to save themselves from the full emotional impact of what they know. And what is it that they know? I quote Rascovsky and Rascovsky (1972):

> The sadism and cruelty to children of parents and other social institutions are denied and converted into justified anger at parents or their substitutes, such as society or the gods, for the supposed or attributed iniquities of the children. The fact is that the aggression of the children was originally instigated or caused by the persecutors. Once again we are compelled to conclude that the stressing of the parricidal accusation is another form of filicidal action. The parents' fantasies and acts of abasement or abuse of the children are thus transformed by the children into self-blame [p. 275].

To maintain self-cohesion under the weight of such knowledge is difficult; to maintain a respectful psychoanalytic stance, even harder. When I began to understand more fully what incest really means, why the barriers against it are so important both for society and for the individual, I began to appreciate Ferenczi's pioneering work more fully and gained respect for his formulations, which had come about within the context of a very incomplete analysis with Freud. I would like to emphasize once more that, while I was and am fully convinced that revelation of my feelings in an analysis is in most cases counterproductive, I do believe that both feeling and thinking have to take place in both partners in the psychoanalytic dyad. Thinking and feeling in tandem includes the deciphering of nonverbal cues the patient gives to the analyst, often without being aware of it. Sometimes these cues turn out to be from the preverbal past and are even more difficult to deal with than the first category of cues. Yet, they may contain important traces of early conflict or, conversely, alert one to the presence of conflict-free spheres that speak to the innate strengths of the patient.

NONVERBAL COMMUNICATIONS

Until recently, not much attention was paid to the nonverbal communications of analysands, let alone analysts' somatic responsiveness—and this despite the rapt attention of the pioneers of psychoanalysis to what McLaughlin (1992) has called "the complexities of the behavioral dance and somatic music that accompany the poetry of human communication" (pp. 152–153). The central place in all psychoanalytic interventions was always assigned to the spoken word. After all, Freud had constructed a model of rational man. Although he also hypothesized a body ego and was himself an astute observer of bodily manifestations of conflict, he ascribed such matters to human infancy and to psychic primitivism. Following him, psychoanalysts have tended to look at nonverbal behavior as an inferior form of communication that has to do with primary, rather than secondary, process.

Yet, in resonating with our patients, do we really employ only our rational mind? Many recent publications on countertransference speak to the contrary. Regression in the service of trial identification is nowadays practically a given in the treatment armamentarium of many psychoanalysts. And this always includes, and sometimes even assigns the most important place to, bodily phenomena that alert the analyst that something is at work in the countertransference. I am speaking here in particular of Jaffe's (1986) illuminating work about how musical clues come to mind when he listens; to Jacobs's (1973, 1986) exquisite sensitivity to the minutest gesture while listening; and to McLaughlin's (1992) inspired use of his kinesthetic-affective responses in resonating with his patients. And I have become comfortable with some of the idiosyncracies of my own listening stance. For instance, I have noticed that, when I did not really like a patient, I would in my tracking reverie place him or her in a beloved landscape, such as the ocean or the mountains. This defensive maneuver helped me to attend to these patients in an empathic mode until I discovered the source of my dislike.

The all-important stimulus to somatic and other kinds of countertransference is, of course, an analysand's material, especially when it is connected with infancy. Greenacre's (1941) evocative description of "mirroring" prodded psychoanalysts into thinking more and more about what she saw as "a kind of visual and kinesthetic introjection of those around the infant. The child reacts with a puckered, worried or tense expression when the people around it are cross or gloomy" (p. 49). Similarly, some analysands respond to the analytic situation and their analysts with specific nonverbal cues. These cues are often shaped by the transference, symbolizing the distant past. The question once again becomes when and how to include bodily phenomena into the psychoanalytic process. Many formulations were constructed about early infancy and its influence on psychoanalytic theory and practice. Some were based on the observation of patients during treatment, others by direct observation and research with infants and children. Kernberg's (1975, 1976) and Kohut's (1971, 1977) schemas relate to the former; Mahler's (1968; Mahler, Pine, and Bergman, 1975), to the latter. It is not within the scope of these introductory remarks to review all the insightful and helpful observational data from direct infant and child research. Suffice it to say that Roiphe and Galenson's (1981) work on the early infantile origins of sexuality was an eye opener for me and substantiated some of my clinical findings, namely, that loss of body boundaries accompanies the fear of annihilation. A quarter-century earlier, Bela Mittelman (1954, 1955, 1957) was concerned with motility, casting it as a drive. Interestingly, none of these investigations offered a suggestion on how to use the discovered material as interpretations. In my opinion, ignoring nonverbal communication also has to do with the psychoanalytic preoccupation with the spoken word. Yet during the second year of life "there is a level of organization in which communication is based on a sign-signal interchange, and a discrete sense of self and the other is internalized" (Lichtenberg, 1983, p. 193). I reasoned that for a good many of my patients this toddlers' level was developmentally intact and therefore offered a safe haven to which they could regress defensively when repression, disavowal, and denial no longer worked.

Perhaps it was the panel on "Nonverbal Aspects of Child and Adult Psychoanalysis" (Panel, 1977) that set the stage for

further acceptance of nonverbal behavior as important communication to be understood and interpreted. In essence, the
panel held that

> the advantage of the verbal system lies in its explicitness and easy
> notation, but as Freud commented, the nonverbal communication is
> there for us to discover if we are attuned to its appearance. The latter
> has wider and deeper range but is more diffuse, since the messages
> are being emitted from multiple sources. In total communication,
> complementarity is involved, with each modality proffering a com-
> mentary on the other [pp. 694–695].

Margaret Mahler, on the same panel, thought that the significance of nonverbal communication was best learned by
observing children during their first 18 months, when nonverbal language development occurs on the basis of sensorimotor
intelligence. She wondered about the resistance among analysts to "even cautious interpretation of nonverbal communication deriving from this early period" (p. 704). Cecil Mushatt
added that "superficial analysis could result unless primitive
identifications, symbolizations of organs and body parts as represented in the body posture, were analyzed and integrated
into the new ego" (p. 704).

Because I was trained as a dance therapist[1] before becoming
a psychoanalyst, I hailed these contributions as the theoretical
cornerstones that would allow me to integrate what I knew
about the communicative aspects of bodily phenomena into

----

[1] Psychoanalytically oriented dance movement therapists assume as a basic
given in their work that all life's vicissitudes imprint our bodies. They base
this assumption not only on empirical observations but also on the work of
Schilder (1950), who formulated that

> there is so close an interrelation between the muscular sequence and the psy-
> chic attitude that not only does the psychic attitude connect up with the mus-
> cular states, but also every sequence of tension and relaxations provokes a
> specific attitude. When there is a specific motor sequence it changes the inner
> situation and attitudes and even provokes a phantasy situation which fits the
> muscular sequence (p. 208).

Sandler and Joffe's (1967) hypothesis of the tendency to persistence in psychological function and development also assumes the existence of early—
that is, somatic—memory. The most important cornerstone of psychoanalytically oriented dance moment therapy as I have developed it (Siegel 1984),
however, is the closeness of body ego to nonverbal behavior in Mahler et
al.'s (1975) research on development.

my psychoanalytic work (Siegel, 1984). I did not then, and do not now, find of psychoanalytic significance the work of Laban (1969), who developed a way of notating movement qualities. Derivatives of this mode of observing patients, such as Kestenberg's (1967) movement profile, also leave me dissatisfied because they reify into objective data phenomena that are, in essence, subjective and dependent on their context for understanding. Rather than noting the frequency and quality of a given bodily behavior, I was always interested in what such often unconscious actions were saying within a given context. The context here is the psychoanalytic situation, with its restrictive use of motility, which sometimes fosters gesticulation, mimicry, unusual postures, fidgeting on the couch, and even borborygmi (Da Silva, 1990). Above all, no interpretation about bodily motion made within the transference-countertransference dyad is valid if it does not include the patient's perception of it. Not only preconscious memories but transference aspects and defensive behavior can be seen in patients' motility. A ubiquitous example: the patient who appears to associate freely in the prone position while hanging one leg from the couch and firmly planting it on the floor, ready for flight. If the analyst does not include observation of such behavior in interpretations, much conflictual material will go underground again, perhaps never to surface again. Psychoanalysts align themselves with resistance and repression if they listen only to verbal communication, even if they include awareness of affect and mood.

I have found that the nonverbal actions of a patient on the couch often open the door to memories otherwise hidden. This is true especially of very early or very traumatic experiences such as incest. Kramer (1992) in this context speaks of "somatic memory" of incest: "These are bodily sensations that occur well into adulthood and are most often accompanied by great displeasure, aversion, or physical pain during foreplay, intromission or coitus" (p. 151). Elsewhere, I (Siegel, 1984; Siegel, Voight, and Voight, 1996) have referred to similar phenomena as "body memories." They were present in most of the analysands I will introduce here. It became apparent that during their travail they sometimes had to give up ownership of their bodies in a regressive way in order to survive psychologically. Obviously, I had to reconstruct, with the patients' help how this state of affairs came about.

RECONSTRUCTION

I am well aware of the pitfalls of undertaking reconstruction and was often tempted to ignore what I perceived in favor of Brenner's (1971) sensible admonition that psychoanalysis presupposes the capacity for verbal communication. Yet Greenacre's (1975) formulations about the central place of reconstructions were a beacon for me. She saw in her clinical work that constructions "may arise either in the mind of the analysand or in that of the analyst" (p. 697) and eventually, in the joint work of patient and analyst, "lead to sound reconstruction, usually enunciated by the analyst" (p. 701). For her, verbal communication was also the most important channel through which "real knowing can be achieved" (p. 703). But she included many nonverbal and preverbal communications in her interpretive work. She observed:

> These are matters of posture, restlessness, special muscle tensions, changes in facial expression, blushing, interferences with speech, changes in tone of voice, lacrimation, sweating, excessive salivation, weeping, urinary and defecatory pressures, changes in respiration, sighing and so forth and so on . . . they . . . indicate that the current anxiety contains quite specific regressive pulls to preverbal troubled conditions in the early period between the total dependence on preverbal language and the acquisition of speech [pp. 703–704].

Fortunately, she was not the only well-known analyst to have included reconstructions of such early happenings in her work. Per Roar Anthi's (1983) paper on the reconstruction of preverbal experiences also gave impetus to building bridges between somatic and psychological memories. Reconstructions of preoedipal times by way of observation of derivatives from the distant past are by now common. As Blum (1977) has made us aware, Freud himself included preoedipal dimensions in his reconstructions, as in the case of the Wolf Man, who experienced the primal scene at age 18 months. Although Freud regarded this incident as a traumatic sexual seduction occurring in preoedipal times, he did not think that it was immediately significant. "Invoking the concept of delayed trauma as a possible explanation, Freud proposed that the preoedipal primal scene became pathogenic as a phase specific oedipal trauma at the time of the Wolf Man's nightmare on his fourth birthday" (Blum, 1977, p. 759). It is practically impossible to reconstruct such early happenings without taking into account what might have taken place on the sensori-motor and motility levels at that time, especially in view of the extensive research into the early origins of human psychological development by Mahler et al., (1975), Lichtenberg (1983), Stern (1985), and others.

But I did not have to go to research alone to justify inclusion of bodily manifestations, including sensori-motor and movement aspects, in my interpretive work. My own clinical experience informed me that patients' memories of such events as incest are frequently preceded by sensory hypersensitivity of one kind or another or by preferred body stances and gesticulations that disappear once recall is more or less complete. As McLaughlin (1992) puts it:

> the older emphasis on the regressive and primitive significance of the nonverbal component of human communications . . . has only slowly been challenged by a developmental viewpoint that would ascribe to primary process modes a continuing importance for all aspects of human behavior [p. 154].

But, in view of the recent research, we need to discuss whether or not the two-year-old who still communicates most of the time in a sign-signal mode is doing so under the sway of primary process. Where and when the so-called secondary process evolves has become an open question with as many answers as there are researchers. Those who psychoanalytically treat patients formerly thought to be unanalyzable have come to recognize that they must at times try to decipher nonverbal cues as though they were already part and parcel of symbolic processes. Psychoanalysts who deal with the victims of incest must surely do so even if their patients are not in the famous, or infamous, borderline category. As Valenstein (1989) points out "very early experience tends to be recapitulated through affectively colored reenactments in the transference rather than through verbalizable memories or reminiscences at a secondary process level" (p. 441)

But these are formulations that have only recently gained respectability in psychoanalytic circles. Greenacre (1975), for instance, had to defend herself against charges that her reconstructions were "really constructions, imaginative speculations

which I had impressed on my patients" (p. 694). But her formulations and those that followed are enormously helpful, and
they need to be incorporated in the analyst's listening and
interpretive stance when treating the aftermath of incest.

INTERPRETING THE UNSPOKEN

There seems to be no agreement among psychoanalysts about
what is interpretable. Since Kohut's (1971, 1977) path-break-
ing formulations regarding the treatment of people afflicted
by narcissistic disorders, there has even been dispute about
what constitutes an interpretation. He favored empathic reconstructions in adult analysis without reference to the important
infant research I have cited. Yet infant research provides the
foundation for including nonverbal and somatic communications in interpretations (Lichtenberg, 1983; Roiphe and
Galenson, 1981). But Kohuts followers have rather successfully
bridged the gap between the empathically recorded data of
adult reconstructions and infant research. For instance, Tolpin
(1980) gives another slant to the observation of babies when
she conceives of them as innately smiling and happy, only
resorting to aggression when unduly frustrated. I found these
newer hypotheses helpful when I was confronted with patients
who were intensely unhappy and often confused. In trying to
deal with the ambiguities of the ideal analytic position, I caught
myself more than once scanning for evidence of positive
experiences in people who had been cruelly misused. I could
not imagine how else they had managed to stay functioning for
so long and so well without somewhere along their developmental way receiving adequate nurturance. I am still not quite
sure if these thoughts belong in the category of therapeutic
intent, countertransference, or attempts to keep difficult analyses from derailing until genetic interpretations, including
reconstructions, can be heard and processed.

As I mentioned earlier, many of these analysands seemed to
fall back on very early somatic memories either to gratify themselves or to stave off further fragmentation. These regressions
appeared to be filled with such intensely private matters that
could not be communicated to me verbally. The signal from
analysands, then, was most often: "Stay away from me." The

bodily behavior, for example, the posture on the couch, suggested relaxation, sometimes even relative comfort, that appeared to exclude awareness of the surrounding setting. I felt not so much defended against as simply not perceived. It then became a question of what this distancing behavior meant.

DISSOCIATION

I clearly was in the presence of altered states of consciousness in such cases, but at first I did not understand what these states could mean. On one hand, I was disregarded; on the other hand, some of the patients knew that there had been an interruption during the analytic hour and were willing to talk about it. They even referred to it as though they had just experienced a "little refreshing snooze," or a "crazy, sexy, absence from you but with you there," or "my mind floating away from my body, not a bad feeling, really." Together, we were in each case able to understand what these dissociations meant. While all these phenomena constituted some form of dissociation, they meant something different to each patient. Therefore, I am once again unable to agree with colleagues like Davies and Frawley, (1992), who postulate a dissociation of an internal "screaming core of a wounded and abandoned child" (p. 16) for every one of their incestuously abused patients. They stress that they do not wish to interpret the appearance of the "dissociated child-self [which] has a different ego structure, a more primitive and brittle system of defenses, a fuller and more affect-laden set of memories" (p. 21) but try to "encourage temporarily the evasion of responsibility" (p. 15) in order to "enter" the dissociative experience of their patients. For them, entering through their countertransference into the dissociation is the "royal road" to otherwise unavailable, split-off experience and memory (p. 15). That dissociation can contain split-off memory and defend against discovery is partially true; the dissociation itself, in several of my cases, turned out to be a bodily, or somatic, memory of one or another aspect of the incest per se! Davies's and Frawley's theory, however, appears to revolve more around splitting and isolation than around dissociation, unless I misread their case illustrations. To reiterate my own position: dissociation is not always a defense but can be part of a somatic memory.

Shengold (1989) offers a partial explanation for how such states, which he calls autohypnosis, can occur. He believes that autohypnosis occurs as a result of "the ego's need to defend against drive tension or to further their discharge" (p. 141). What is defended against is not the transference or anxiety-producing memory but the drives that were overstimulated, possibly by incest. Shengold's formulations are closer to my clinical experience in that they address the possibility of a partial enactment of incest during dissociation, which provides an avenue for discharge while disguising itself as a defense against transference. The observation of incongruous bodily behavior on the couch can alert analysts that an enactment, not a resistance or even a defense, is taking place. Because dissociation as enactment includes drive discharge, it can be gratifying and can therefore prove analytically counterproductive. If, however, analysts remain aware of the potential for misreading dissociation as resistance only, they will not find it difficult to include its other aspects into their interpretive work. Perhaps the usual reading of dissociation as resistance only (Fliess, 1953; Dickes, 1965) will have to be broadened to include "dissociation as enactment of trauma." This hypothesis is amply illustrated by the cases of two women whose histories are of particular interest because they grew up in families where incest was not only transgenerational but multigenerational.

Chapter 2
Multigenerational Incest
—Mrs. Raphael

I t is a psychoanalytic commonplace that parents who sexually abuse their children were themselves abused. That this
form of sexual transgression is transgenerational goes
almost without saying. Transgenerational usually means that a
member of an older generation breaches the boundary of someone younger. But, if the parents were incestuously abused, obviously the grandparents were also involved. To my knowledge,
no published report of such a multigenerational aberration
exists in the psychoanalytic literature. I feel both privileged
and intimidated by the responsibility for reporting on two cases
in which grandfathers had primed their daughters to accept
incest as a basic given of life. These daughters became the
devouring mothers of the two women whose case histories I
will try to present here. Both women at a certain point in their
analysis felt it imperative to find corroboration for their memories. One, Mrs. Raphael, the subject of this chapter, called it
her "fact-finding mission" and indeed found an uncle who corroborated her memories. The other, described in the next chapter traced down "two witnesses." Mrs. Hutchcombs's "witnesses" were a physician who had treated her mother as a
youngster in distress and an older stepsister of her mother who
seemed relieved to share her knowledge about the family dynamics from which she herself had fled. No doubt remained
at the conclusion of these analyses that the mothers of my
analysands had been incestuously abused by their own fathers.
They, in turn, became the sexual abusers of their children.

What startles me is that there were so few similarities between
Mrs. Hutchcomb and Mrs. Raphael and between their dysfunctional families. The families, though, had this in common: they

were outwardly intact and held themselves superior to their neighbors in comportment and in the manners expected of the children who were to become my patients. Their income levels and societal expectations also were similar in that they lived modestly in relative financial security and valued sons above daughters. Otherwise they were dissimilar in ethnic background as well as in the way they coped with the guilty secret, the denial of which seemed somehow to be a stabilizing feature in one family while the other one simply seemed to accept the chaos created by the pater familias.

Besides their need to test reality, my analysands shared dissociation as a partial enactment of their traumata; they suffered depressions, sexual dysfunction, curtailed object relationships, and at times, sexual identity confusion. Yet, the outcome of their analyses was very different for each. One told me toward the end of her analysis that she had "righted her life." The other left feeling bereft of her childhood illusions and unable to mourn the loss of both her idealized mother image and her analyst, whom she had experienced as protective. She decided to stay in a sterile relationship that afforded her little pleasure but promised "safety."

Mrs. Hutchcomb's and Mrs. Raphael's treatments were separated by a time span of 10 years.

Though complaining of confusion, depression, and anxiety, Mrs. Raphael was able to give a reasonable account of her life. She had been in group and individual psychotherapy for seven years when she decided that she would like to enter an analysis. She had read that "this is a way to make yourself over." The members of her group and her therapist had strenuously opposed her decision to look for an analyst. Despite their protests, she consulted a locally prominent psychoanalyst who, because he had no time open, sent her to me. She was upset by "being handed around" but remained, determined to find a therapist who would attend to her needs. In her group sessions she had felt "swallowed up and not seen or heard." At the same time, she experienced support and had made friends with several members of the group. Her therapist had encouraged these friendships because, according to Mrs. Raphael, they were all unable to form friendships "outside," meaning outside the group.

Mrs. Raphael acknowledged that she had gained a great deal from her therapy and that it had opened her eyes to certain "irregularities and strange scenes" in her family background. In particular, she had felt strengthened by the support she received after giving birth to a little girl, now six years old, and by the insights she had gained about her difficulties in her marriage. She was relieved to hear that she could not possibly be the only one at fault for incessant quarrels. She had constructed a cohesive narrative about her life and used this narrative as a lens through which to judge present feelings and events. For instance, her recently deepening depressions, frightening dreams, and recurrent headaches did not seem consistent to her with the image the group had helped her build. She did not feel herself to be the "shy but charming mother, wife, and teacher" the group saw. She thought there might be parts of her like that, but right now she felt "guilty, ashamed, controlled, and convicted by the group." She could not say how she was controlled or of what crime she was convicted. She just knew that she had to seek a different form of help in which she did not need to be "Miss Sunshine for other people."

Her narrative revealed her to be the oldest of three children. Her brother was five years younger than she and had been a problem all his life. Her father was an actor and was frequently on the road with one show or another. One of the traumatic incidents Mrs. Raphael remembered clearly was the night her brother was born and she, then five years old, had to make the phone call to have her mother taken to the clinic for delivery. Because the father was absent and her mother did not recover quickly from the birth, the screaming infant became his sister's responsibility. "I felt that I had no childhood. I never had time to play. I had to take care either of the baby or of my mother, who was never really right. She always picked quarrels with everyone we met and yelled at my father when he was home. He never spoke back to her. When my younger sister was born, he was home but he was disappointed that she was a girl. Even though my brother is crazy, they always liked him better." The brother was constantly in trouble. School authorities recommended treatment, but, rather than "accepting such a blemish," the family moved to another district. Eventually, the brother was placed in a mental institution and, when he recovered, went to live with a foster family. He visited his own family frequently and was always "received like the prodigal son. The calf was always slaughtered for him. We girls got nothing," Mrs. Raphael reported. She was both ashamed of her family and in desperate need of them.

Mrs. Raphael's mother acted increasingly irrational, buying boys' clothing for the girls, picking quarrels with the neighbors, and forbidding her daughters to play with anyone who did not first pass muster with her. When the father was out of town, mother took the children to bingo halls, where she "lost all track of time and let us wander around by ourselves. She made friends with these down-and-outers and then expected us to be nice to them. She also drove them to places, and we had to visit these places, which stank of sweat and urine." Father, when told of the situation, did nothing. Both sets of grandparents tried to help but were harshly sent away. In particular, the mother's family tried to intervene, sending their youngest daughter, Nina, over to look after the children. Both daughters went to Catholic schools, where they did well. The nuns were especially pleased with the intellectual development of Clarissa (who was to become Mrs. Raphael, my analysand). But Clarissa was constantly uneasy, afraid her mother would make a scene or issue yet another restriction on her activities. She had become "gross," a very overweight young girl who longed for the attention of her peers, particularly boys. She was very fond of the young aunt who often came to visit. Clarissa tried to be vivacious and pretty like her but did not succeed. When she was 13, she made a devastating discovery: Nina was not really her aunt, but her half-sister. When Clarissa's mother became pregnant with Nina at age 15, the family took in the infant and raised her as one of their own numerous children. The father was unknown. Nina confided all this to Clarissa when, at a very early age, she contracted uterine cancer. Nina died shortly after her confession to Clarissa, who was as stunned by her death as by the revelation of Nina's origin. She was not able to mourn Nina until she entered her previous therapy.

During her analysis Mre. Raphael referred to Nina as "that piece of sparkling ice inside of me." During the analysis, Mrs. Raphael described how, after the shock of discovery, she had felt even closer to the young woman and angrier at her mother for not acknowledging her own child. She also feared that there might have been something wrong with her parentage. "Somehow" she grew up, managed to go to college, and became a special education teacher, the first in her family to earn an advanced degree. She met her future husband at school and thought "they would be happy forever after." He was the only man she had ever gone out with. She was "thrilled that anybody wanted me." But soon trouble started. The young couple were not sexually compatible. Mr. Raphael accused his wife of being a wanton who needed too much sex, while she was repelled by his body odors, his sleepless pacing at night, and the thick cigars he had smoked since their marriage. It was then that she sought the help of the therapist whom she had just left.

THE BEGINNING

Mrs. Raphael entered each session as though she were deeply afraid. Head bent, eyes looking toward the floor, she would walk rapidly to the couch, peruse it quickly, throw one covert glance at me, and then settle herself down, staying nearly immobile for the entire session. She seemed unaware of what she was communicating nonverbally but came in with an increasingly emotional agenda. Although she had readily agreed to the ground rules, such as using the couch and number of sessions (four per week), she became upset that she could not see me while she was on the couch. On the other hand, she did not wish to sit up because she was afraid I might think her "too crazy" if she did so. She very quickly established a volatile transference in which I was experienced as alternately all-powerful or as totally deranged. She never responded verbally to transference interpretations but seemed to use them as a cognitive beacon that allowed her to stave off an as yet unknown peril.

She lamented the absence of physical holding and hugs in the analytic sessions and said they had been part of her previous interventions. On closer examination, it became apparent that these hugs had been dispensed by members of her group when they met outside the sessions, not within them. We examined the difference between a hug given by a friend and a hug dispensed as an intervention. Tears came to Mrs. Raphael's eyes. "You mean to tell me we will never hug each other?" she cried, as though this were news to her. She then enlarged on her objections to analytic abstinence and at the same time accused herself of being too confused to understand what was going on. She continued to show regressive transference yearnings, wishing that I could be her mother and give her all the things she had missed in childhood. What things? "Like being told the truth about who is whose child," she said bitterly.

The obfuscation of her older sister's true status took center stage for quite a while. Mrs. Raphael traced her inability to follow a map or to retain verbal instructions as quickly as to written ones to her mother's denial of her oldest daughter. A particularly frightening symptom was that she sometimes arrived at a place and did not know how she had gotten there, or she found herself talking to people she could not recall having made plans to meet. She felt that these occurrences were also linked to her mother's denials. This symptom invaded the analysis as well. She confessed that she often immediately forgot what I said and wanted me "to talk more so that she could remember more."

But she also wanted me to admire her and to love her like my own child. She thought "an analysis is the second chance around. So when do I get my second chance?" She had fantasies of wanting to move in with my family and me. "But even if you permitted it, which you probably won't, I would still be the outsider, as always," she commented bitterly. She developed a highly erotized mother transference in which she beseeched me over and over again to hold her in my lap, to nurse her, or to help her get away from her husband. She was unable to take in interpretations and began instead to make advances to a girlfriend she had known since childhood. The friend warded her off, stating, "we did the let's-play-doctor-thing when we were kids." Mrs. Raphael felt deeply hurt and derided. "It's your fault if I turn out to be homosexual," she said. "You should tell me what's right and what's wrong, not sit there and say I yearn for a good mother. Of course I yearn for a good mother. I never had one. And my father doesn't know how to be a father either."

In the midst of shame at having acted out her needs, Mrs. Raphael nevertheless found it possible to verbalize intense feelings of deprivation and despair of ever having enough warmth and mutuality in her life. She was certain that she did not want anything from her husband—"a lost cause," she claimed. She wanted an intense and gratifying relationship with a woman.

But it had to be a woman whom she could trust,. like her analyst. Otherwise she might be open to the same kind of humiliation she thought her girlfriend had meted out. But instead of
acting out again, she began to deal with her transference feelings by accusing me of being "too seductive and mysterious in
my silences."

Simultaneously, she began to feel strong enough to tell me
another well-guarded secret: before she learned that her aunt
was her sister, she had exposed herself to her brother, asking
him to stroke her. He declined, and she became so furious at
him that she beat him. Now that they were both adults, she had
apologized to him and he had forgiven her, she claimed. She
recognized the intensity of her feelings in the analysis as similar to the intensity of feeling when she tried to seduce her
brother. She had fantasies about becoming a boy herself through
sexual contact with her brother; she bitterly expressed phallic
yearnings around the thought that her parents might have liked
her better if she had been a boy. She also "hated herself" for
having added to the already heavy burden of her emotionally
disturbed brother and wondered if she was like her mother,
"congenitally unable to restrain myself."

At the same time, she took another look at her relationship
with her young daughter and realized, with a shock, that she
had left management of the child's care to her husband. "I don't
want to be like my mother, so I thought, I won't be a mother at
all," she sobbed. She also noted that her husband and her
daughter had become "a couple who keep me out," repeating
aspects of her own oedipal drama in which she had at times
merged with her father as the gentler of her two parents and
thus became the caretaker of the fecund mother whom she
assisted in giving birth. She understood that, in her effort not
to be like her mother, she had in part identified with the parent of the opposite sex and his sex organ. An identification
with her little daughter, whom she envied, also came to light.
She wanted to be the well-beloved child both of her analyst and
of her husband, the same husband who was so inaccessible to
her as a wife. On a cognitive level, she began to appreciate the
many double binds she found herself in: she was a mother who
forbade herself to mother in order to save her child from herself; she was a sister to a woman whom she thought to be her
aunt; she was a sister who tried to seduce her brother, whom

she had nurtured as though he were her baby and with this behavior displaced her mother as a partial oedipal victor. It was at this juncture that Mrs. Raphael began to report dreams. This also was the beginning of a long discovery and working-through process that at times strained my inner resources. But by the end of the first year the transference had deepened sufficiently for Mrs. Raphael to focus on the defenses that had helped her to survive and adapt to a painful reality. I felt that in large part it was possible for Mrs. Raphael to start reflecting about herself because I kept a tight reign on my countertransference.

Some entries in my notebook.[1]

> Mrs. Raphael is appealing. She looks like a Putte, one of those androgenous angels of baroque painting and sculpture, a little pudgy, pouting, full lips, too much black curly hair, precariously teetering on high heels like those stucco angels that hang, but appear to be falling, from the ceilings of Italian palaces and duomos. Just as hard to see and to relate to, also. One invariably has to strain one's neck in order to see the angelic smiles and pouts. She never looks straightforward at anything except the couch when she first walks in . . . . reminds me of putus—a lad. Aren't those adornments called "il putto"? But in Spanish a puta is a prostitute, if I'm not mistaken. What's going on here? So far, no more than the usual evidence of bisexuality and unresolved Oedipus. Sometimes a borderline flavor. Her life history is too smooth, as though she created it to cover up something. Or is that only the result of being told what to think and do by her group? Certainly she talks about them as though they were inquisitors. But that seamless life narrative . . . . I feel I'm sliding on its surface without a toehold.
>
> The constant nagging and whining is stressful. She certainly sees herself as an "exception." How wearying she is. Here we are at the beginning, relatively speaking, and already I alternate between feeling like a dead potato and outraged on her behalf. I play with the idea of actually taking her on my lap but, instead of feeling anything about so impossible a fantasy, I think of Ferenczi, Freud's anger at him, how I would be drummed out of the society if I allowed such a thing. Mothering certainly comes easier than analyzing, at least to me. Even if the infant is a demanding one . . . . not unlike a colicky baby who never lets mother sleep. She

---

[1] All excerpts from my notebook appear in this sans serif type.

pulls on me in that direction. Why do I need to stop feeling along with her and to think of the ancient quarrel between Freud and Ferenczi instead? What are we both defending against?

Nausea in huge waves. She is becoming increasingly more demanding. To be expected. Borderline? Today, when she finally said she wanted to be nursed I felt nausea. Thinking of that pope, a Medici, I think, who was said to elevate his own progeny to high office and take his own daughter for a mistress. Nursing a baby is pleasurable, very sensuous. And if your baby happens to be a girl, the interaction can be said to be homosexual. But what is sexual here? The sensuality of the satiated baby, or the relief of the mother whose breasts finally are emptied . . . . but I don't think that's what Raphael is after. She lies on that couch like a dead fish, totally immobile, never shifts position. That immobility means something. If she moves she will be—what? Maybe she wants to be my baby because that is a way to ward off danger and instead of making me into a giant boob her intent is really to keep me at a distance because she fears me as she feared her mother. Another body fluid is blood. Bet she fears being drained and therefore wishes to drain me first. That would explain the nausea.

Always the same. The ones who claim to want, to love, to admire the most are the ones who need to kill . . . . still surprises me.

Doesn't want to hear that the attempted seduction of the brother at age 12 must be the replay of something earlier, just as the attempted seduction of her school friend now is an acting out of what maybe happened to her, but with whom and when? Certainly trying to do it in the transference to me . . . .

I misjudged as ego strength her determination to leave her group therapy. It now looks like a search for a forum to restage her trauma . . . . but isn't that what we all want?

Contemplating shifting hours so that I have more time after her sessions to settle down . . . . would that be a countertransference enactment?

THE MIDPHASE

Mrs. Raphael's Dreams and Memories

When Mrs. Raphael began to report her dreams, her ability to reflect on her behavior had already increased. It was not clear at this point whether she had taken a new developmental step and was now able to symbolize more fully or whether it was the establishment of a more positive, less erotized transference that permitted her to use formerly disavowed ego functions in the service of self-scrutiny. Certainly my interpretations were informed by my countertransferential musings about her distorted mother–child relationship. Mrs. Raphael gradually disidentified from the lustful, abusing aspect of her maternal introject despite long periods of feeling dead, uncommunicative, and "not like anything alive under the sun." She had accepted the formulation that her acting out of phallic yearnings with her brother must have been connected with inferiority feelings and narcissistic disappointments suffered in the past when, for the first time, she reported a dream. I had the impression, however, that this was not the first dream she had since the analysis started but that it was merely the first dream she thought to report. She had an idea that dreams "slow me down" and at the same time "would bring me too close to the analyst, with a dangerous kind of closeness." This was her first reported dream: Her husband is in a coma and totally inaccessible. As she looks at him, a nice little dog enters the room and falls apart. A group of people come in and try to help, but they are clumsy and just intrude. It is a big city where everyone is cramped for space. Two of the people say, "You are giving birth." She is sure that they are wrong because she herself is a snake. Her analyst appears, and we all go to the movies together.

It was not difficult for Mrs. Raphael to equate her husband's dream coma with his very real emotional and sexual withdrawal from her. In order for him to have an erection at all, she had to don black stockings and garters and parade around in the nude. Even then he sometimes could not be aroused. He defended himself by shouting insults at her. Often, after failed sexual encounters, he would incite their little daughter, Emma, to say or do something provocative or dangerous. When Mrs. Raphael intervened, both of them would laugh at her. She shamefacedly admitted to screaming and sometimes hitting her fist against the wall when she saw her daughter turn against her. Despite her husband's behavior, she was determined to make a go of the marriage because she was certain that she could never find anyone else. In her view, masochistic surrender was preferable to being alone. She was chagrined to realize that she was even willing to give up her daughter so long as she could remain the titular wife and mother. To her, being alone meant being overwhelmed by feelings and fantasies that she thought would drive her mad. Worse than madness, she feared behaving like her mother.

The dream also helped us to examine how much Mrs. Raphael dreaded crowds, or, rather, groups of people who could possibly manipulate her. She was certain that the people in her dream who had come too close must have been her former therapy group. She waved aside a possible connection and warned to me to keep my distance also. According to her, the dream showed clearly that I only went to the movies with her, didn't I? She thought this was helpful and good and giggled at the thought that her life might "role like a film in front of your (the analyst's) eyes." She thought also that perhaps the little dog who fell apart was herself prior to her first therapy. But how could she be giving birth to herself if she were a snake? She associated "changing skins" and then wailed about her inability to change "in depth." Her changes were only "skin deep." She cited as an example her inability to mother appropriately. At first, she had not even wanted to look at her baby when she was born, but with the help of the therapy group she had managed to take care of the infant. But now she felt herself to be an ineffective, poor mother, glad that her husband took over even if that meant less contact with her daughter.

The snake image as the body as phallus came into focus much later. When I cautiously probed about the self as a snake, Mrs. Raphael felt insulted. She thought I had accused her of being like her mother, who was the "snake in the family, the one with the poison in her fangs." This failure of empathy on my part had serious consequences. Mrs. Raphael slipped into such a rage that she left the session early and in the next seemed lost in a self-protective haze. Poor timing on my part forced Mrs. Raphael to fall back on primitive defenses of withdrawal and splitting. A pattern now emerged in which extreme ambivalence, doubting, and self-recrimination followed in rapid succession. She began to doubt that analysis could help her, forgot to pay her bill, and even forgot to come to some sessions. A couple of times she arrived wild eyed at the time her session was supposed to end, giving accounts of having been lost on the highway or of not knowing where she was.

I conceptualized these happenings as a form of dissociation that permitted her to keep something important in repression. She reactivated her "stupid self" and at the same time disconnected emotionally from the analytic process and her analyst. Despite this inner turmoil and acting-out behavior, her posture on the couch remained stiff and motionless. Her dreams seemed meaningless to her now. She only mentioned that she had them but did not report their contents. Finally, one of the dreams perturbed her so much that she wanted to discuss it although by now she was certain that no one could help her out of her misery and extreme anxiety. The dream was, indeed, filled with troubling material. She had dreamed that her little daughter, Emma, was in bed next to her. They were both naked and indulged in some sex play. It felt good and warm until she was suddenly repelled and had to vomit. She jumped out of bed to check on Emma, who was sleeping peacefully.

Mrs. Raphael once again saw herself as homosexual and now as a pedophile. She genuinely feared that she would repeat with her daughter the scene with her brother. Simultaneously, she began to worry that I might die when I went on the summer break that was then some weeks off. I formulated that her fears had to do both with her introjection of the seductive, abusing mother and with that aspect of her shaky self-representation that had not been nurtured by either of her parents. Despite this turn of events in her analysis, she was able to deal very effectively with a new blow in her life. Her husband lost his job and revealed that he had used all his credit cards to their limit. Without any doubt in her ability to succeed, Mrs. Raphael took over the expenses of the household, sent her husband to an employment agency, and instructed him on how to care further for Emma. When I commented on the contradiction between the fantasy of herself as unproductive and worthless and the reality of her competence, she thought I had praised her. It was the first time that she could fully allow herself to feel the benign neutrality of the analytic situation uncontaminated by the incestuous eroticism that seemed to invade all her other relationships and made her suspicious of her wish to merge with me.

Seemingly as a reward for this fantasized praise, which I conceptualized silently as her acceptance of me as a selfobject (Kohut, 1971, 1977), and perhaps also as a going away present or to assuage her guilt about thinking me dead, she came up with some memories. In the years before her brother was born, her mother and she were often alone, sometimes in unknown cities where they lived in a hotel room while her father performed somewhere. During such times, her mother would be extremely anxious and require the child to come to bed with her until the father returned from his performances. Then she would stroke her and pet her, calling her endearing names, and masturbating her. But when Clarissa started to bounce around in glee and lustful overstimulation, mother would become angry and command her to lie still. Eventually this ritual was called "laying still." Clarissa both loved and dreaded it. Several times she tried to tell her father about the exciting games she played with mother. He had a curious response. He bought her a doll. "He thought I was talking about taking good care of mother, who was highstrung, and the doll was my reward."

Clarissa became confused and thought that maybe she had imagined her interaction with her mother until the same scenario was repeated on subsequent performing tours of her father. Confusion began to play a part in her life from then on. She reported never trusting her perceptions entirely to this day. Her curiously stiff posture on the couch now gave way as we examined the transference implications of this behavior. On occasion, she craned her neck and grinned at me or wiggled her toes when she became excited by her own story. She laughed loudly and heartily when I interpreted the disappearance of her stiffness as a sign that now she was sure I would not sexually misuse her as her mother had. I also raised the possibility that the rigid posture might not only have been a response to mother's order to be still but an unconscious acting out of mother's wish for an erect penis. Again, this brought forth laughter, which later we understood as a defense against understanding what I was saying. During this time, she dreamed of her husband and daughter as hostages but recognized these dream images as representations of herself and her brother.

A volatile period then ensued during which Mrs. Raphael could tolerate neither my emotional availability nor my absence. Like an overstimulated child, she raged about things she could not control. In particular she was incensed that I did not curtail my summer break in order to help her through her difficult time. She hated her body, wanted a breast reduction performed while I was gone, and threatened to find out where I would go and to follow me there. She again thought of herself as homosexual and found it difficult to cope with her oscillating body feelings of sexual greed and hatred of her sex organs. Eventually, she associated that her breasts represented the bad child and the bad mother as well as bad sex. These fantasies of self-mutilation and homosexuality revealed themselves as partial identifications with the abusive mother, who had used her child's body as though it were part of her own.

At other times, Mrs. Raphael felt quite literally that her body did not belong to her. She described herself as "floating somewhere that should be pleasant but isn't." She began to doubt again that her recall was correct. "Nobody's mother is that crazy, not even mine," she declared. States of dissociation occurred more and more frequently on the couch. She would suddenly lie stiff and still, a corpselike pallor covering her. Then she would either moan or giggle. On occasion, she would bounce her rear up and down and then cover her mouth mirthfully. She always knew when she had been "absent" but could not always recall what she had experienced. Sometimes these episodes were followed by strong guilt feelings; at other times she appeared exhilarated. When she herself noticed the differences among the affective states that followed her autohypnotic absences, I interpreted them as the somatic memory of maternal incest, which consisted of sometimes lustful, sometimes painful masturbatory intrusions by the mother.

Mrs. Raphael slowly came to understand that she had been her mother's "plaything." "I think I ranged in importance somewhere between a dildo and a toilet," she said bitterly. Despite these memories and the turmoil of her emotions, she faithfully visited her parents each weekend, always coming back with tales of insult or ridicule. Her mother wanted her to divorce her worthless husband and to abandon her analysis. With a shock, Mrs. Raphael realized how strong a symbiotic hold her mother had on her. "She acts like I'm still her lover," Mrs. Raphael said. She toyed with the idea of confronting the old lady but feared the consequences. "Supposing she dies? She has high blood pressure. The shock could kill her. I'd never forgive myself!" She then described herself as "almost dead, tied to mother, being mother when I want to be myself."

Mrs. Raphael squeezes the analytic life out of me. I have to fight sleep whenever she regresses into her enactments. Silesia, with its white farm houses and healthy animals is often, in my thoughts. I even placed her in the farmyard in order to be able to listen to her better. How strange this dark curlytop looks among the blond Hünen.[2] Except there weren't any Hünen in Silesia. When she told me about her mother masturbating her, I felt as though someone had punched me in the solar plexus with an iron glove. Totally breathless, like a huge weight on my chest. Does she feel like that? I remembered those children I wasn't allowed to play with because they might be the offspring of incestuous unions. I felt chilly and like trembling when I listened to Mrs. Raphael. I also felt like going to sleep and not dealing with her twisted fantasies. Why do I place her among Norsemen? To show myself that even in the places I love I could not love her? Must be something about Thor, the thunder god who would strike you dead with a thunderbolt. . . . I feel stuffed with guilty secrets and transgressions I should be metabolizing for her. . . . Mrs. Raphael's treatment is like being hit constantly with thunderbolts. I feel like killing her mother, or like encouraging her to confront her. So far, I've managed to keep on an even keel, analytically speaking. Images of the Krystall Nacht in Berlin, myself under grandfather's desk. . . . I think the Hünen imagery was instead of Nazis. Couldn't quite face them again, the Nazis, or neutralize and contain all that aggression, hers and mine.

When she cranes her neck to look at me, I feel as though she has caught me in a masturbatory act. That's it. She's pushing that stuff into me. I feel like she must have felt. . . .

More Dreams and Memories

Slowly, Mrs. Raphael began to cope both with her overstimulation and her need to deny what had occurred. Although the states of dissociation persisted, they were less frequent. She dreamed that she was in an attic, trying to match up babies with their mothers but didn't know how to do it. I appeared on the scene and insisted that she did know who belonged to whom. When she tried to hand the babies out, she gave the right baby to each mother.

Her associations at first led to her brother. Apparently she had tried to seduce him again after she was married. This time,

---

[2] Hüne is a German word for giant man. The word was derived from the Middle High German Hunne and is related to the name of the nomadic riders who swept into the Gothic empire from Asia in 400 A.D.

he had agreed to look at her and to tell her what he saw. When he had an erection, they both became frightened and dressed, but not before he had commented on the fact that she was a "beautiful, round person, a woman." Her brother had not been to see her since that incident. Her fantasy was that if her husband found them together, he would respond differently from the way her father had when she told him about her mother. Her husband would protect her. She realized that she had pushed her husband into the role of a parent and wondered if that had affected their sex life adversely. There seemed to be little shame tied to this incident about exposing herself to her brother as opposed to the earlier one. Curiously, she did not associate her sister to the dream image of babies having to be matched with their mothers. Instead, she declared herself pleased with her brother's recognition of her as a "round woman." This incident brought to my mind the time when she thought I had praised her when, in effect, I had only mirrored her (Kohut, 1971). This mirroring had affirmative and integrative value for her, whether it came from her brother or from me. Object constancy seemed far off at this point.

Mrs. Raphael had arrived at an omnipotent denial of responsibility. She now wanted to be given to by everyone. She expected reparation and immediate gratification from me, from her family, and from fate itself. This proved to be a formidable resistance. The expressed feelings of narcissistic entitlement and power were hardly to be influenced by interpretation. She was certain that I shared some of her omnipotence because I had correctly interpreted some of her dreams. Therefore, she felt that I "knew that it wasn't her fault her family was crazy." Far from mourning the childhood she never had, she embarked on a search for affection and gratification from me. She wanted me to rescue her and not let her "simmer in the stew of her rotten life." The old demands for symbiotic union surfaced with great strength though unaccompanied by dissociation.

Mrs. Raphael's reactivated grandiose self seemed to swing between yearnings for oral-tactile gratification and extreme sarcasm about all and sundry. Nevertheless, she did not entirely absent herself from her analytic commitments. Slowly, Mrs. Raphael allowed analytic examination of her own aggressive impulses and adaptive responses to her trauma. My countertransference had been useful in cautioning me to just how cruelly this woman judged and punished herself, as though she were the presiding Nazi executioner of her growing self. To escape such harsh feelings, she had to split off temporarily what was most painful to her, namely, that she had on some level participated willingly in the abuse and had even passed it on. She was reluctant to see herself as seductive, even though she had tried to entice her brother into incestuous behavior. In her fantasies, it was not her fault. She had merely acted like her mother, trying to get rid of unpleasant body feelings. At first, she did not seem to understand that this was an identification with her mother, whom she consciously despised. Some time later, she could accept the fact that she acted out of a need to turn the passively experienced trauma into active mastery. "Some mastery," she snorted. "Why would I want to act like that old harridan?"

Despite her apparent disavowal of this interpretation, her defensive structure loosened sufficiently to allow a barrage of memories to surface. Her maternal grandmother died when she was 14. An opulent funeral took place with a large dinner party afterward. Mrs. Raphael and her mother were the only members of their nuclear family to attend. Father was on the road, brother was in a hospital, sister was with a babysitter. Nina, then still alive and well, had seated herself with the children of the dead woman. Clarissa felt betrayed. Nina should be sitting with her and her mother; she belonged to them! After everyone left, the grandfather asked Clarissa's mother to stay for the night. He was afraid to be alone, he said. The mother agreed, on condition that Clarissa could also stay. She was surprised that grandfather asked her mother to comfort him instead of his other daughters or sons. Everyone in the huge clan knew that Clarissa's mother was capricious and given to eccentric behavior. But no one said a word when the old man invited this daughter to comfort him.

When Clarissa got up at night to go to the toilet, she passed grandfather's open bedroom door. There she saw her mother in his arms—they were making love. Revolted, she vomited into the basin in the bathroom. The noise caught her mother's attention. She grabbed Clarissa by the hair and ordered her not to say a word to anyone. Somehow, Clarissa managed to creep back into her own bed, beset by trembling and fear. When she reported this memory, she shook and trembled on the couch, could hardly speak, and pulled on her hair, once again choosing physical activity to express her conflict. I told her that she did not need to do to herself what her mother had done to her, that she did not have to succumb to her mother's mode, and that together we would try to understand the impact of this event on her life as we had tried to understand her other memories.

After she recovered this particular memory, Mrs. Raphael's amnesia for many childhood events lifted. She recalled the times when her mother packed her three children into the car to take them to bingo halls and then abandoned them to wander through empty school buildings or church basements. After the bingo sessions, mother would take people home and stay up drinking coffee or alcohol with them, not bringing the children home until the early morning hours. On occasion, the children witnessed scenes of alcoholic shouting and weeping, of people defecating and urinating. "But it wasn't as bad as seeing grandfather in bed with mother," Mrs. Raphael said. "There were three of us, and we held each other and played or sometimes we slept on dirty couches or on beds or on the floor."

It seemed as though Mrs. Raphael now measured everything that had happened in her life against the enormity of the incestuous behavior of her mother and grandfather. Even her own incestuous abuse by her mother paled in comparison with this discovery. She became depressed and doubted everything she did. When she kissed her daughter, she wondered if that had been too sexual. She excused her husband's reluctance to look for a job on the grounds that being married to someone like her was enough of a job for anyone. She dreamed of babies who were cold and had no clothes, of fathers who were supposed to protect their children from robbers but didn't, and, finally, of a rapist who stalked her and who was really her mother.

The transference became charged with suspicion. When I wore a dress with a full skirt, she thought that I wanted to "flounce the skirt at her and seduce her." After that session she dreamed that she was at an abortion clinic all day but nobody helped her to get rid of the unwanted fetus. Finally, a doctor drew it out, but it wasn't a baby. It was something else. Mrs. Raphael interpreted this dream herself. She thought I was the doctor who "drew everything out of her." She accused me of being a tease and a seductress, then apologized for her behavior, apparently wanting me to order her to leave the room. She confessed that she wanted to leave analysis and that she hated me. During such times, she seemed to lose the "as if" quality of the analytic process even more than during her act-ing-out and acting-in bouts, seeing me as the actual incestu-ous, dangerous mother. However, somehow she always managed to pull herself together before the end of the hour and punctu-ally appeared for the next session to traverse the same terri-tory over and over again.

Eventually, another transference dream helped her to neu-tralize at least part of her distress. She dreamed that she was in labor and spilled blood and water all over the floor. Even though she was in pain, she had to clean it up by herself. Then her analyst appeared with a boat on a serene lake and told her that she could have the boat for recreation whenever she wanted it. Mrs. Raphael cried when she reported this dream and talked about her gratitude to me for "accompanying me through my hell." She understood without interpretation that she "was giv-ing birth to myself and had to do that" and "that the boat had something to do with calm and pleasant vaginas."

Nevertheless, even after all the analytic work and successful reconstructions, she still doubted that these events could be true. "Shouldn't I be mad, or raving in a hospital some place instead of talking to you about it?" she asked. Despite the ago-nizing self-doubts and the unpredictable swings of the trans-ference, Mrs. Raphael's agitated depression gave way to inter-pretation. Her ego consolidated sufficiently for her to swing into action. She decided that she needed to go on a "fact-find-ing mission." While I was aware that such reality testing was important for Mrs. Raphael, I also interpreted it as a continu-ing mistrust of the analytic process, the transference object, and her own perceptions. An important change followed; Mrs. Raphael let go of her guilt about having seduced her brother and her fear that she would repeat this seduction with her daughter. This working-through process allowed her to sort out blurred internalizations of her daughter as her sister and of herself as a carbon copy of her mother.

The maternal clan was gathering to discuss a matter that, during the volatile time of remembering and working through, seemed of little importance to Mrs. Raphael. Belatedly, the family had commissioned a headstone for the grave of her sis-ter Nina. The headstone had been in place for some time but had not been paid for because alterations had been made in its inscription without the consent of the clan. Mrs. Raphael's mother had ordered them without consulting anyone. She had had her dead daughter's last name changed to her own married name, thus finally claiming the dead woman as her own. I did not think that it was a coincidence that this symbolic act of taking possession occurred while Mrs. Raphael was busy trying to free herself from the symbiotic clutch of the older woman. While the family gathered and argued, Mrs. Raphael asked the oldest of her aunts if she knew who Nina's father was. She didn't, she said. Mrs. Raphael kept pressing her for details of Nina's birth and finally asked straight out if grandfather had been the progenitor. The aunt gave a startling answer: "If such a thing had happened, it certainly wouldn't have been with your mother. She was disruptive and ugly and disturbed. He would have chosen me if he had wanted such a thing. I was the prettiest of the sisters."

Mrs. Raphael had sufficient analytic understanding at this time to realize that her aunt had verified an incestuous atmosphere. She decided to talk to the one of her uncles who seemed the "steadiest" to her. She made a date to visit him at his house. She had always liked this uncle because he was jolly and played with the children. She regretted that she saw very little of him. He usually visited the family only on Christmas or at important family functions. When she visited him, he corroborated her memory. As a high school boy he had been called on by his mother to watch his sisters. He at first did not know what he was to watch for but soon found out. To his horror, his father regularly took one or the other of the sisters into his bedroom. When he confronted the old man, he was beaten and crudely told to leave the house, which he did at the earliest possible moment, returning only after both his parents were dead. Further, he told Mrs. Raphael that her mother had been a very pretty though hard to handle child. The mother had refused to go to school, talked back to everyone including their father, and finally was severely punished by having to sit under the table while the family ate.

This information once again plunged Mrs. Raphael into an affect storm (Krystal, 1978). But her inner structure was no longer as labile as it had once been. She questioned the very intensity of her feelings and discovered their overwhelming strength to be a response to her mother's interference with her perceptions. She began to understand what she repeated in the transference situation, namely, the denial and repression not only of the many incestuous traumata but also of the affective states and defenses surrounding the traumatic relationships and their meaning.

> My revulsion nearly makes me sick. Becoming enmeshed with the multitude of primitive relationships this woman carries inside of her is not helpful to her. If they blow me out of my chair by the strength of their lustful aggression and brutality, how must she feel? How can I build bridges for her? No, how can I help her to build bridges to her own understanding. She is a valiant soldier . . . . but am I a valiant guide in this impossible odyssey? Too much of this smacks of the self-righteous brutality of Hitler's brown shirts. . . . I can barely breath at times. Whoever invented this bullshit about the detached analyst? I'm certainly not one, but I wish I were. Sometimes I feel like jumping out of my skin, (whoa, hold it! Those are Mrs. Raphael's body memories.) Is the breathlessness a reflection of the patient's seduction? Still, I don't believe I have let anything spill over into her sessions. I am grateful for sitting behind her . . . . imagine having her see some of my feelings. I'm sure that would be the end of the analysis, too much of a burden for her to realize that I am furious with her mother, beyond furious with her grandfather on her behalf. An old truth . . . . but to recognize it once again is humbling. It's almost too much that she sometimes seems to know how I feel . . . . although this may merely be a self-protective function for her, that is, when I'm in a good mood I will not hurt her like her mother hurt her. She often comments on my "mood," though I try to stay on an even keel despite becoming enmeshed with the imagoes rising out of the unconscious of both of us. I noticed several times that allowing her to vent her feelings without comment, probing, interpreting—by my just holding still—the heavy erotic, aggressive, or whatever atmosphere is disarmed. Asking questions seems to make me into the abusive, reality-distorting mother. Yet I also feel that she must live her affects as Ferenczi described. How to reconcile?

WORKING THROUGH

Not surprisingly, this turned out to be a very long analysis. It lasted nine years. The tentacles of the many incestuous happenings reached into every area of Mrs. Raphael's splintered self. In addition, the pervasive atmosphere of terror and unpredictability created by the multigenerational violation of the laws of society among her relatives made Mrs. Raphael's ability to test reality uncertain. Even after her fact-finding mission was successfully concluded, she seemed helpless about what to do with the information she had unearthed. Once again, she hid behind a shroud of pseudoimbecility. On one hand, she wanted to know and did know what had occurred. But the maternal injunction not to know was still strong. Mrs. Raphael found a compromise by questioning the meaning of what she knew and, with a pathetic air, asking, "But why should it bother me if my grandfather was a beast? Maybe I just dreamed it" or "My mother was so lonely. She didn't know what she was doing. I probably just fantasized it all. You're an expert on fantasy. Don't you think I'm fantasizing?"

Dissociation once again surfaced as Mrs. Raphael suddenly found herself in places without knowing how she got there. During sessions, she occasionally would forget where she was and then emerge from her semitorpor with a start and ask, "Am I really here? In your office? I don't know where I thought I was, maybe with my grandfather? Or my sister? Sometimes I think I must live for her." Eventually, Mrs. Raphael discovered that during her autohypnotic dissociations she lived part of the seductions by her mother she most dreaded: the lustful "prickling, good feelings in my, you know, my genitals. It's like I know I shouldn't have them but I do anyway," she explained.

Intrapsychic changes did not take place until the incestuous experiences had been worked through over and over again, tracing their fantasy- and reality-derivatives into as many areas of Mrs. Raphael's life as possible. The interpretive elaboration of the multiple transference reenactments of seduction and terror I have described helped Mrs. Raphael to look at her persistent overstimulation and the various ways she had coped with it. One of her primary defenses had been to "shut down and make believe I didn't know and nothing happened." The working-through process lasted five years, during which Mrs. Raphael was busy with the "righting of her life," as she called it. This righting included a new understanding of her mother. At first grudgingly, then whole-heartedly, Mrs. Raphael began to see her mother as a victim like herself and tearfully abandoned the idea of ever being able to have "a healthy relationship with her. She is too damaged. But I can feel sorry for her without letting her interfere with me any more."

During this period she weathered another storm, namely, the dissolution of her marriage. Her husband could not tolerate her renewed efforts to build an intimate relationship and left after a vacation they had planned as a "renewal." Initially devastated that she "could not even hold this man by her side," she soon discovered herself to be attractive to other men. She obtained another advanced degree, saw to it that her daughter entered therapy, and eventually settled into a more satisfying relationship with an older man whom she had resisted for a long time for fear she might "use him as a father figure without sex."

The separation period was prolonged. We dealt with an upsurge of the need to see me once again as the neglectful, seductive, and controlling mother. Minor disappointments in the hour were seen as catastrophic events. But Mrs. Raphael eventually became able to mourn not only the end of her analysis but also the destruction of her childhood. She needed to stay in touch by phone and letter for a long time after the formal conclusion of the analysis as though to assure herself that both she and I were "okay in the best sense of the word."

DISCUSSION

Mrs. Raphael's body boundaries were impaired by the unwanted repeated sexual overstimulation by her mother. Deeply ambivalent, full of hostility and denial, the mother was unable to provide a stable holding environment for her children, in particular Clarissa. She acted as though her young daughter's body were part of her own, designed to provide her with the satisfaction she craved. In addition, masturbating her daughter to the point of frenzy allowed her to pass on the passively experienced seduction she herself had suffered. This identification with the aggressor was a defense Clarissa introjected and used often. The adult Mrs. Raphael still searched for an omnipotent object who would tell her that all was well, that she did not need to feel guilty or "dirty," so that she could maintain her denial, disavowal, and repression. The strongly sexual transference that arose at times did not at first have the sensual quality women exhibit when they are in analysis and trying to cope with the essentially nonverbal time during which their mothers ministered to them as babies. As Wrye and Welles (1989) demonstrate, the reliving of this early time is "rooted in mother and baby's earliest contact, it manifests itself in con-

crete transferences to the real parts of the body of the therapist; its expressions are typically inhibited as preverbal and/or
defended against out of shame and fear of humiliation"
(p. 683).

My clinical experience with women informs me that Wrye
and Welles's formulation is correct (Siegel, 1994). Once the
maternal erotic transference is recognized, it can be dealt with
like any other transference. The difficulty rests in including in
interpretations such bodily phenomena as flooding tenderness
for the analyst, fantasies of being bathed by her, and so forth.
Mrs. Raphael eventually reached this stage. But, as I have
recounted, whenever memories of either her exposure to the
incestuous primal scene or her own incestuous experiences
came close to the surface, she needed to suppress awareness of
the painful lack of empathic closeness with her mother and
defended herself by sexual demandingness. Both in and out of
the sessions, she needed to act out her conflict through symbolic psychodramas and communicative motor movements. An
example of the former is the attempted repeated seduction of
her brother; the latter became apparent in her stiff posture on
the couch, which served to bind the negative, abusing mother
transference. The aggressively sexual transference she at times
exhibited seemed to be a compensation for the empty hours
when her mother actively forgot her children and left them to
their own devices late at night when she played bingo or was
involved with following her own driven needs. It was as though
she had forgotten all about her children. Furman and Furman
(1984) describe this type of dysfunctional parental behavior as
intermittent decathexis of the child (p. 432). This kind of non-
recognition engenders fury in the child who is decathected
and can lead to a combination of ego defects such as impaired
reality testing and cognitive deficits despite adequate intellectual endowment.

This was certainly so for Mrs. Raphael. Given the oscillations
of being out of her mother's awareness and then being
overstimulated by her, it was impossible for her to develop a
coherent self-image or even a cohesive body ego with reliable
inner-body sensitivities. She did not know whether she experienced pain or pleasure, whether she was being devoured or
was the devourer herself. I hypothesized that, even prior to
being used incestuously by her mother, Clarissa must have had
difficulty in traversing the separation-individuation phase.

Overstimulation of a child's genitals produces its effects early in development and interferes with appropriate development (Mahler, 1965). Her occasional sexual identity confusion and coercive doubting (Kramer, 1983),[3] as well as occasional autohypnotic absences, could also be traced to an identification with a mother who herself had been unable to mature psychically.

Mrs. Raphael, however, had a strong need to succeed, to know who she was and what had happened to her. Born with strong endowments, she was creative in the use of her dreams, intuiting their disguising symbols and using them after the first year of analysis to orient herself vis-à-vis her memories. It was often my impression that she trusted her unconscious more than her perceptions of reality. She courageously took chances in trusting first her analyst, then her own perceptions.

Her primitive needs aroused strong countertransference reactions in me which were marked by colorful imagery which often informed me of affect storms (Krystal, 1978) to come. I had not yet learned to decipher more completely such echoes in my psyche. Nevertheless, because my answering fantasies were most often rooted in my personal history and often occurred just before Mrs. Raphael had one of her emotionally charged episodes, they became particularly helpful in my attempts to stay emotionally available but neutral; thus self-analysis provided helpful warning signals. In particular, preparedness for Mrs. Raphael's volatility helped me to interpret the disguised derivatives of her many traumata and their enactment in the transference. The doubt and confusion that was fostered by her mother's oscillating attitude toward her and her father's actual and emotional unavailability entered into the countertransference as somatic responses. Doubts about whether I could build verbal bridges to Mrs. Raphael's nonverbal remembering also entered the picture and alerted me to the necessity for staying cognitively as well as emotionally ready.

The analytic biography Mrs. Raphael left with was a far cry from the smooth narrative she arrived with. Informed by psy-

---

[3] Kramer (1983) distinguishes object coercive doubting from the doubting of the obsessive-compulsive individual as follows: "Patients coerced the maternal object or her substitute to argue one of the opposing sides of the child's intrapsychic conflicts" (p. 331). The doubting had to do with knowing and not-knowing maternal incest.

chic as well as historic truth, she felt she could "trust herself now to keep doing the right thing for herself and her daughter without putting anyone down." Compassion for her unfortunate mother entered the picture relatively late. It was accompanied by the ability to mourn the end of the close interaction with the analyst and the lack of parenting that had marred her life.

Chapter 3
Multigenerational Incest
Mrs. Hutchcomb

During our first interaction, Donna Hutchcomb requested psychotherapy specifically focused on the sexual troubles she was experiencing in her marriage. She accepted my explanation that I do psychotherapy in a psychoanalytically oriented way. She asked few questions and assured me that she had "checked on my reputation" and therefore was willing to go along with any approach I chose. A tall, handsome, woman clad in fashionable but classic clothing, she had a commanding manner. Hair cut in a short, mannish style was the only discordant note struck in an otherwise pointedly feminine appearance.

She was an executive in a major computer firm and described herself as "doing well." Mrs. Hutchcomb also presented me with an apparently seamless life history. She had married at age 33 at the urging of her family, who were upset at having an "old maid" for a daughter. Her husband was someone whom she had known for a long time and had dated on and off. A civil servant, he also "did well." She had some doubts about him, notably that he "had been single and eligible even longer than I." But when he accepted her religious persuasion and did not ask her to change to his denomination, she took this as a certain sign that he was in love with her. Both were Protestant, he an Episcopalian, she a Lutheran, both deeply religious and devoted to their parishes.

Apparently Mrs. Hutchcomb had had many suitors, none of whom met the ideal she carried within herself. At 14 she had fallen in love with a local boy who was "above me socially." On the advice of her mother, she had kept him at arm's length in order to "stay out of trouble." The young man pursued her until they both reached college age. He had been away at a prestigious private boarding school during which time an idyll formed between the two young people. They wrote regularly and met clandestinely whenever he was home on vacation. In the meantime, Mrs. Hutchcomb as teenager was popular. She was a cheerleader for her high school's football team, something her family appreciated very much. Both parents came from families that "had seen better days" and were eager to rejoin the country club crowd from which lack of money supposedly excluded them. Mrs. Hutchcomb's mother expected her daughter to make a splendid marriage and was her major confidant and adviser in matters of career and marriage. While the older woman felt demeaned by her husband's middle-level position in a large firm, she dreamed of riches for her only daughter. She advised against becoming intimate with Matt, the young boyfriend, because this would diminish her daughter's marriageability. Apparently the small exurban town they lived in was still ruled by the values and social stratifications of an earlier epoch.

Mrs. Hutchcomb imparted this information with amazing conviction. She did not seem to question her mother's view of the world, even had made it her own so that some behaviors of her friends and colleagues seemed inexplicable to her. For instance, when Matt married a girl before he finished college because she was pregnant, Mrs. Hutchcomb felt betrayed by him and was convinced that her mother had been correct. She would have had to enter into marriage "disgraced" and pregnant had she continued her love relationship with Matt. Her mother felt that college was unsuitable for her daughter, although three younger brothers received higher education. This was the only parental decision Mrs. Hutchcomb questioned. She also admitted to detesting all three of her brothers, who had "come to nothing" despite their education, "married beneath them," and teased her unmercifully as a teenager. She now saw that a college degree would have helped her climb the corporate ladder more rapidly and felt bitter that she had been excluded.

Her husband was against her enrolling in night school to obtain a degree because he wanted a wife who was home as much as possible. He did not, however, want her to leave her

lucrative job. After their lavish wedding, Mrs. Hutchcomb discovered that her new husband, John, had a life plan. They were
to live on her salary while he saved all of his money toward an
early and comfortable retirement. Mrs. Hutchcomb had
expected to have children and to stay at home to raise them.
She called herself too cowardly to fight John and, in the service of peace in the family, acquiesced to the plan. She admitted that she shared John's fears that their children might "turn
out poorly and be nothing but trouble anyway." She suppressed
an occasional thought that it was unusual to plan for retirement at age 35 and before establishing a family. She was surprised to find that their home and all their possessions,
including her car, were in his name only. When she discussed
this with her mother, she was told that this was John's way of
taking care of her because she was scatter-brained and not very
trustworthy. Mrs. Hutchcomb did confess to a penchant for
expensive clothes and fine cars but obviously was no scatter-
brain. The responsibility she carried on her job proved this,
she thought. Despite all her efforts to see "the brighter side of
life and how fortunate she was," she had become increasingly
depressed about the lack of sexual fulfillment in her marriage
and now sought my help. In doing so, she felt intensely disloyal
to both her husband and her mother, who felt she was merely
being self-indulgent in seeking therapy.

Mrs. Hutchcomb gave me this information as though it were
her gospel; she was unaware of any contradictions and was
impervious to my cautious interpretive attempts. She was clearly
in search of another idealized object like Matt, her mother, and
her husband. On occasion, she apologized for the triteness of
her life history and in almost obsequious fashion characterized
me as "at the height of [my] career and incredibly smart, probably bored with such a silly life story." She predicted that she
would bore me because "nothing ever happened in her life."
An idealizing transference (Kohut, 1971) soon formed that
made it almost impossible for me to offer anything but the most
trite acknowledgments of Mrs. Hutchcomb's needs. These either were not heard by her or were accepted with awe at my
acumen. She became mired in detailed recountings of daily
events in her office, then called herself to task so that
she could talk about "what I'm here for." These admonitions
reflected her husband's frequently voiced complaints that

therapy took too long, that there was nothing wrong with her, and that she was spending "his" money foolishly on nothing.

She also dreamed frequently but dropped these dreams in my lap without trying to understand them. This lack of interest seemed to be not an inability to associate but a resistance to giving up her idealized version of having a wonderful family. "Being too free and easy with words can lead into real trouble," she repeatedly declared when I tried to examine with her why she withheld or censored so many of her thoughts. It became clear that anyone who in any way became emotionally close to Mrs. Hutchcomb was automatically registered by her insecure self-image as a perfect person.

She did not appear surprised, or even interested, that her dreams portrayed a great deal of violence. At first, she dreamed of a huge, red-haired man with a large belly and even larger testicles, but with a tiny penis, who deposited large amounts of sperm in a hole above Mrs. Hutchcomb's head. Another dream portrayed a red-headed robber breaking into an antique treasure chest, while yet another one dealt with a small pet that turned into a huge Doberman that wanted to tear her to shreds. Given the sparsity of her associations, I did not venture to interpret anything but asked if she perhaps had noticed that her dreams were in stark contrast to her other perceptions. Yes, she said. She had noticed. But so what? Dreams, according to her, were of no substance and had no meaning. But my careful persistence did seem to make an impression. She informed herself somewhat, read a book about dream research, and began to acknowledge that dreams could serve a discharge function, though she wondered "what in the world an ordinary person like myself could possibly want to discharge."

Almost despite herself, Mrs. Hutchcomb allowed her pondering to lower the wall against what she had so long been unable to talk about, namely, the reason for her presence in my consultation room: the unsatisfactory sexual relationship with her husband. She blamed herself entirely for not being able to respond to him. She thought the fact that she being a virgin at 33 had contributed to pain she felt during each intercourse. A gynecologic examination had not shown anything abnormal, and so she was sure that she was doing something terribly wrong. As she kept describing what actually occurred in her bedroom, however, it became clear that her husband "does not believe in too much foreplay. It is too lascivious and makes him uncomfortable." He entered her without making sure that she was lubricated. She shamefacedly admitted that on occasion she did feel "wet," but never in relation to her husband, only when she thought of Matt. She also admitted to comparing notes with some women friends who were "always wet." She begged me to tell her if this wetness was a normal feature of sexual arousal. When I asked instead why she thought her responses abnormal, she was unable to answer. Nevertheless, my question had made an impression. She once again sought out the library and there found the information she wanted.

This independent activity in the service of reality testing emboldened her to turn her new knowledge into action. She managed to persuade her husband to pay attention to her responses. Overjoyed at first, she found that her elation soon turned into gloom. She was unable to reach orgasm, and her husband again accused her of being unresponsive. But by now Mrs. Hutchcomb knew how to use the library and, by reading more complex sex manuals, discovered her husband to be a prematurist. He ejaculated as soon as he entered her. They discussed the matter, prayed together, and decided to bring their problem to a series of marriage encounters sponsored by their churches. Having reached a conclusion that she said satisfied her, Mrs. Hutchcomb thanked me profusely and ended her therapy. Convinced that we hadn't even begun to scratch the surface, I assured her that my door would always be open to her. Our interaction had lasted a year and a half. Two weeks after her departure, Mrs. Hutchcomb sent me a basket of roses and a thank-you note.

> She is absolutely right. I am bored to tears, have to fight the urge to go to sleep. On the other hand, there is something so touching about her naivete that it keeps me involved at the level of a kindergarten teacher. A very, very injured lady who is frightened of unleashing her grandiosity. What became of the healthy exhibitionism of the cheerleader? At the same time, I am sure that there is a cauldron beneath that controlled behavior. Acts like a narcissistic personality disorder but, if this were so, would she have this kind of dream, packed with sexual innuendo, violence . . . . old Ferenczi is raising his head, I think. Before Kohut, maybe we would have just called her an as-if personality. On the other

hand, the one genuine response I had from her was because I endlessly reflected her demands and tried to be sympathetic to her many injuries. That mother sounds like hell on earth. And the husband is a recapitulation of ma. Wouldn't be surprised if he has red hair.

The red roses: would like to send them back. That would injure her too much. So she sees me as her lover? Or as an abuser? No wonder I was bored! Defending against seduction? No, not NPD [Narcisstic Personality Disorder]. Incest comes to mind. Why? The hole with sperm above her head and all the injuries of the box, etc.?

MRS. HUTCHCOMB'S ANALYSIS

Three years later, Mrs. Hutchcomb reappeared. Looking pale and exhausted, she claimed to be ready for an analysis "no matter what." She could not explain why she felt depressed and exhausted now because her life had become "better than ever." Both she and her husband had been coached in their marriage encounters on how to achieve a harmonious sexual relationship. Mrs. Hutchcomb found that she could reach orgasm when her husband permitted her to take the position on top of him; he learned to masturbate before intercourse so that he could maintain an erection while satisfying his wife. While they at first enjoyed this very much, they soon become "tired of all the work involved; after all, they had busy work schedules and had to get up early in the morning, "too early to indulge in sex all the time."

But Mrs. Hutchcomb had finally found pleasure in sex and was not to be deterred from seeking satisfaction. She courted her reluctant husband, who managed to elude her. She found him masturbating in the bathroom for his own pleasure, not as a prelude to intercourse. Profoundly insulted by his onanism, she accused him of "spilling his semen on the earth. The bible forbids it." After this episode, she sought help from her minister, who instructed her in positive thinking. From a Catholic girlfriend, she learned about affirmations, which, she felt, reinforced positive thinking. She got up half an hour earlier every morning and practiced her affirmations and prayed for her husband's responsiveness.

Gone were her self possessed style and her smooth delivery of words. She spoke through clenched teeth and toward the end of the first hour confided that she suffered from temporal mandibular joint syndrome and was on an antidepressant. She was already in treatment for her jaw when she heard that Matt had gotten married for the second time. This news threw her into such an uproar of headaches, abdominal cramping, and crying that she went to her family doctor. He had a ready diagnosis: early menopause. Her periodontist advised the removal of some teeth for reasons she could not grasp, and her husband increasingly cloistered himself in the bathroom "to pray." In addition, he revealed himself as "unnecessarily clean and neat. He vacuums the rug in the bedroom every morning before work because there is fuzz on it from my cotton underwear." Much to her dismay, she had become furiously angry with him for always blaming her. That's when she remembered "how protected I felt in my psychotherapy "and now wanted" the very best, the deepest—an analysis." Of course her husband objected. She no longer cared. "I don't love him at all any more," she shouted. We managed to schedule four sessions a week notwithstanding Mrs. Hutchcomb's shock at her spontaneous outburst.

Mrs. Hutchcomb saw herself as a model patient. Early on she flushed her medications down the toilet and declared herself ready to investigate her past. During the years after she left psychotherapy, she had done a good deal of reading and understood intellectually what a commitment an analysis is. She was overawed by her own courage to make such a commitment without any reinforcement from her mother and against the wishes of her husband. I saw her need to be perfect at all times as a defense against possible abandonment. Despite the relatively high level of her ego organization, her defensive system consisted of more primitive mechanisms, such as projection, body language, physical and mental avoidance as well as action instead of verbalization.

Because she was fixated on overestimated, narcissistically cathected objects—especially an archaic mother imago—I did not in the early stages of the analysis interpret her defensive structure, preferring to stay with empathic reflections about her feeling states in the here-and-now in order to give her time to establish a less impoverished self-image. The atmosphere in the analysis was such, however, that naivete as a manipulation became the issue. For instance, she wanted me to praise her for her choices while at the same time showing me how angry she could get at her boss, her mother, her husband. Being angry was a feeling state she thoroughly enjoyed. She had never felt this way before, she claimed. When I asked if she thought her new-found anger would please me, she was puzzled. Wasn't it her job to develop new ways of conducting her life? Further-more, she thought it downright unfriendly of me to be so silent. She had committed herself to the analysis despite all obstacles, but she was not at all sure that I was as committed to her.

She often reiterated how upset she felt by my silences. They made her feel that I was indeed bored by her and that she would have to work harder to keep my interest. She felt both ashamed of her "plain Jane life" and angry that I could not be her best friend. She kept pressing me for details of my family life and wanted information about my leisure activities. When this information was not forthcoming, she felt abandoned and shut out. At the same time, she felt that my silences "spoke volumes." As gently as I could, I asked her if she could identify the con-tents the volume of books she was referring to. This partial interpretation made sense to Mrs. Hutchcomb.

She gradually gave up acting like a supplicant and began to deal with her first true insight. It occurred when she noticed that her jaw did not hurt her when she shouted at other people but that it began to hurt again when she and her husband said their prayers together. He, probably to rescue himself from this newly aggressive wife, had become involved in a ministry to the old and infirm, which required him to spend many evenings away from home. Mrs. Hutchcomb wondered why God did not let her be free of pain when she was praying to him for release and mercy. "Maybe it is evil, after all, to be angry with people," she said. Despite such immersion in her religion, Mrs. Hutchcomb did not give up "being angry" but continued to assert herself.

A decision had to be made about the removal of teeth to cure Mrs. Hutchcomb's supposed TMJ syndrome. She sought a second opinion and then decided "to fire both those bastards," meaning the dentists. Again she expected praise for her actions and literally pouted when none was forthcoming. After this incident, the transference shifted to an alter ego fantasy; that is, Mrs. Hutchcomb entered into a sort of twinship with me (Kohut, 1971) in which she saw both of us as similarly endowed and as able to "conquer the world." She endowed me with inor-dinately high levels of energy and success and simultaneously wondered where she herself suddenly got so much energy. "Maybe it had to do with all the energy spent on the teeth. I think I used to get angry with my teeth," she offered on one occasion. Her self-consciousness and shame, somatic language, and depression temporarily gave way to excitement and an anxious grandiosity, during which she declared that she would quit her job and study psychology or law, or would become a physicist like Matt. This tenuous identification with a phantom lover and the shift in the transference temporarily helped her to shore up her uncertain self-image. Her grandiose self had been reactivated and displayed itself in the sort of momentary brilliance that a psyche populated by idealized figures can spawn.

> I sometimes wish she would fire me too. Even when she appears to associate, she doesn't. Something so hollow I cannot touch . . . . Must keep a tight ship and not fall for the pull to mother. What are my own needs vis-à-vis this prototype of all NPDs? Feel like telling her to get on with it and tell me the secret already. What secret? What are we colluding about? It's clear she wants to be loved on her own terms, but who doesn't? Last session she was talking about being angry with her teeth—I had that symptom. Couldn't breath and felt my stomach turning. No hint so far of incest. Impatient because she can't get to it just yet? Feel like telling her what it takes to be a physicist. Why am I so angry with her? She has shown some ego strength; the work is coming along. Must be because she has no idea I'm in the room with her.

The Midphase

Mrs. Hutchcomb reported success on her job but continued failure with her husband. Enmeshed in her dreams of glory, she hardly registered John's withdrawal as significant. She was thrilled to find admirers among both male and female co-workers. She felt ready to plunge into an affair with a much younger man when she again dreamed of the man with the red hair, huge belly, and testicles. In this second version, the man's penis had shrunk even further but was dripping some sort of liquid. It wasn't clear whether it was blood or semen.

Instead of associating to the dream, Mrs. Hutchcomb suddenly wanted to talk about her relationship with her mother, who now expected the young couple to attend family dinners once a week. Mr. Hutchcomb did not like them very much but, as a devout Christian, felt it his duty to comply with the wishes of his in-laws. Mrs. Hutchcomb did not like these mandated family sessions either and noted that her new self-esteem faded considerably when she was confronted by her mother. Mother felt "left out and pushed aside" by both her son-in-law and her daughter's analysis. While mother tried to reestablish her power base in her daughter's life, the men drank beer together until they were in a stupor. Both women would then join in attacking their husbands for their behavior. This made both of them feel superior and reunited. Suddenly it occurred to Mrs. Hutchcomb during the session that her mother had red hair. She could hardly bear to examine the dream of the man with red hair, claiming that it had been too long since she had dreamed it. But she was also intrigued and began to compare her slim, attractive mother's physiology with that of the partially bald, fat man whose genitals were so out of proportion. She reported in subsequent sessions being "haunted by this creature. Sometimes I think it's my mother when she was pregnant with my brothers. But it couldn't be she. She has no penis. Suppose it is my husband? But he is a fanatic about his figure. He works out on the stationary bike each day and goes to his health club three times a week. The small penis would be right. But it's not really small; it just doesn't work right. And then he blames me when sex is no good."

Nevertheless. she found several parallels between her mother and her husband. They were both "bossy" and wanted her to do everything their way. "I don't love either one of them," she declared. Wanting to take this statement back as soon as she had made it, she exhorted me to "forget it." Following this session, she reported always feeling tired, without energy once again and "not there. It sounds funny and strange not to be there. If I'm not there, where am I? Doesn't that sound funny? Or is it crazy?" At work, she found it hard to make decisions and ended up staring out of the window. Clearly, she was depleted by her attack on her internal image of the two people she had formerly thought so powerful. She noted that the pain in her jaw had reappeared but was no longer fixed in one place. When she spoke about either her mother or her husband, it traveled to her throat. It became so intense that she could speak to me only in a whisper.

I formulated that in the past she had perceived her mother and her husband as fused into a single powerful supply of protection and love, but now they were no longer able to sustain her. Mrs. Hutchcomb responded with a flood of memories she could not tell me quickly enough. Her oldest brother was born when she was three years old. When she saw her mother nursing the baby, she became so angry and upset that her mother let her "take a swig."

Her mother called the baby's penis "a lolly," much to the confusion of her daughter, who thought lollies were lollipops. She fantasized about sucking on the baby's penis but was repelled by the odor of urine, or so she reported as an adult. She had expected the baby to smell of milk and that somehow the penis would contain milk that she could drink. When the other boys were born, her mother smilingly reminded her daughter that she had been allowed to nurse as well. When the little girl became angry and felt put down by such reminiscences, her mother laughed even harder. Mrs. Hutchcomb now professed to hate all three of her brothers. That was why she and her husband went to see her parents by themselves without the rest of the family present. "She doesn't invite the boys and their slutty wives when I come," she told me. "We can't talk when they're around. They are uncouth."

After much hesitation, Mrs. Hutchcomb revealed that the oldest of her brothers, the one with whom she had shared mother's breast, was in jail and had been there several times already. She described him as the most intelligent of her brothers, one whom she had sometimes protected against her mother's unpredictable rages. He had grown up to be equally enraged with his own children, whom he regularly beat until visitation rights were withdrawn after his divorce from "that slut who added to his problems." Mrs. Hutchcomb had a fantasy of rescuing her nieces and nephews, of taking them to live in her house and showing the whole world that she could be a good parent. Of course, her husband, against this move, pointed out to her that the children would have to turn out to be trouble and in trouble because of their father's record. Mrs. Hutchcomb was not pleased with the way she had handled this crisis. She spun fantasies of visiting her brother in jail and magically transforming him into a good man, husband, and father. Primary in these fantasies was the wish to be commended and praised by large numbers of people for her outstanding devotion to her family. My praise was no longer elicited.

She had begun to play with her fantasies in yet another way. A steady visitor of her local library by now, she had found a book that showed naked women and one that reproduced 49 positions in love play, supposedly from a Chinese collection. Mrs. Hutchcomb fantasized herself to be the favorite concubine of a Mandarin. But while she depicted to herself the joys of such a role, her throat closed up and began to hurt again. She feared that she might be homosexual. Didn't the dream of the redhaired man show that she had no idea how men and women were supposed to look? She felt aroused by the pictures of the nude women in the book and thought she might masturbate while looking at them. She decided against doing so because, once again, her throat began to hurt. Besides, she didn't know how to masturbate, she claimed, because as a child, she had never touched herself. She did remember, however, that she had had "shudders" traveling from her vagina to her head. These shudders felt good.

When she was about ten or so, she "finally made a good friend." She went to the friend's house often, stayed overnight, and even spent some Christmases with them because these holidays were "awful at home. Mother shrieked and cried and father got drunk and the boys tore down the house." In the quiet of one Christmas night, the two girls took a mirror and looked into each other's vaginas. The friend did not have shudders and wanted to know how one could get them. Mrs. Hutchcomb did not know what to answer then and still had no answer now.

She was almost always hoarse and spoke in a whisper. She spent many sessions contrasting the calm and orderly household of her friend with her own. Mother was always either sad or complaining about money. She often took her little daughter, Donna, with her to meet father on the days when he was supposed to get his paycheck. Not until she was a teenager did Mrs. Hutchcomb realize that this was necessary because father "had another woman," to whom he gave money. All the children sided with their mother. On the nights father was not home, one or the other of the children slept with mother who was afraid to be alone. When it was her daughter's turn, the mother regaled her with stories about her husband's beating her and how unfortunate she was. Donna had often seen the parents fight but could not recall any scenes of beating. It was clear to her, however, that mother had to be consoled. Mother needed soothing and asked to be stroked.

Mrs. Hutchcomb became very frightened after she revealed these scenes. She suddenly did not know how she had stroked her mother or even that she had stroked her at all. In a dream, she saw a dead person in a coffin on white satin. The person's ear was bleeding. Mrs. Hutchcomb did not know if it was a man or a woman but "guessed" that the dead person might be her mother, her father, her husband, or herself. On the other hand, the person might not be dead at all because there was blood coming out of the ear. She also "guessed" that the dream might be the opposite of what it showed, namely, a birth instead of a funeral, but she could not imagine whose birth was involved. Certainly it did not contain any hope for children, for she felt she had given up that thought.

Everything seemed hopeless and confused to her. She resorted to forgetting sessions, calling up for changes of time, and threatening to withdraw from therapy because it was too expensive. When asked who thought it was too expensive, she readily agreed that it was her husband. But so what? "They were man and wife, wedded together for better or worse." I formulated that perhaps she needed to think temporarily like her husband in order to ward off what threatened to overwhelm her. Sobbing, she agreed that, yes, she needed her husband to help her and to take care of her, especially because I refused to do so. She had hoped I would be her special friend, but I had turned out to be only an analyst.

Besides, the cause of her problems didn't lie with her mother and whatever she did to help calm her mother. Yes, she helped her poor, innocent, betrayed mother, but it was her father who was to blame for it all. He was a violent man. He would sometimes come home and swear and shout and beat his fist on the table. Once, when she was already an adult, he lent her car to a friend of his without asking her first. When she asked for the car back, he threw the keys on the floor and "made her crawl on the floor under the table to get them." She stayed under the table because it was safe. Her mother and she were the victims. Men were useless, violent, and not to be trusted. But her husband, John, was different from father. He did hold her in his arms when she felt bad the other day. They tried sex, and he wanted fellatio but she could not perform it. After all,

urine comes from there. She thought it "ridiculous" that anyone would want to take a "urine spout" into their mouths. She
linked these thoughts to the tight closure of her jaw.

> So that's why I wanted to withdraw from her. My defense sys-
> tem mirrored hers only too well. Been thinking of her as an NPD,
> not at all my usual mode. This really showed me once again what
> a trap it is to let yourself think in diagnostic categories! Of course
> she needs mirroring, but of a different kind than Kohut talks about.
> There seems to be no rudimentary self-love, just a numb (and some-
> times dumb) awareness that she just might be entitled to more
> love, more nurturing, more warmth from just about everybody in
> that family of the unalive (not to say undead!). For a long time no
> idea what I was defending against, sure that it wasn't just the usual
> boredom of being perceived as a turnip or auxiliary body opening
> for the ventilation of ice-air. Great relief when I realize that her
> under-the-table scene isn't so different from my under-grandpa's-
> desk-scene during the *Krystallnacht*. Her father imago sends me
> spinning into those Berlin days, with Nazis beating up old men.
> Somehow, also, the burning buildings during air raids . . . . watch
> for the coming sexualization of the transference. And what's that
> about fellatio and urine? Acting out with husband what had
> already occurred with baby brother? Too early to interpret any-
> thing. And what went on in mother's bed? Maybe the asthmatic
> lack of air I feel these days has to do with incest again. Also indi-
> gestion. A tightness in my stomach . . . . can't stomach what's to
> come. . . .

RECOVERING THE MEMORY OF INCEST

Mrs. Hutchcomb now became diffident and scared. Phobias
and delusions made it hard for her to experience reality, let
alone test it. She was beset by fears of dying in a snow storm,
being attacked by terrorists, being thrown out of an open window. Worst of all, she feared that I would betray her and tell
everyone that she was homosexual. Besides, she was now certain that her father had thrown her against a wall when she
was still an infant. According to her, that's what that dream so
long ago meant. Not that a fat man had put semen in a hole
above her bed but that her father had wanted to kill her. She
knew this was true because her grandparents had told her that
father was too punitive with her, especially when she was a

baby after he came home from the Korean war. He could not stand her crying and was said to have "harmed" her in the belief that this harm would keep the infant quiet. Mrs. Hutchcomb also thought that her crying drove her father away.

She delivered these so-called memories in a high, whining voice that sometimes disappeared altogether. She had daily headaches, broke out in a rash around her mouth, and developed several sebaceous cysts on her scalp. Once again she wanted to leave therapy but decided to stay because she was "too scared to leave with half my life hanging out of my head."

States of dissociation on the couch became frequent. They would announce themselves by heavy breathing. Her speech became incoherent and finally was no more than an attempt to form syllables. Often, she tried to knead the headrest or stroke her abdomen.

Mrs. Hutchcomb regularly awoke from these absences refreshed and curious about what she had said and done. Usually, she also wanted to know something about me. Did I work so hard because I was also trying to get out of an impossible marriage? How was my sex life? For that matter, did I have a husband or a lover? She sometimes was able to laugh at herself because by now she was quite aware that I would not answer her. She said that she had learned to listen to my silences because they were full of meaning; therefore she hoped that her silences (the states of dissociation) also were full of meaning.

A dream brought her somewhat closer to what she was so desperately trying to fend off. In it a couple of condors had only one egg. Mother and father condor fought over who was to take care of the egg and in the struggle kicked the egg out of the nest. It broke into many pieces. Mrs. Hutchcomb associated her maternal grandparents to the condors. According to her, they were of a "better class than my mother and father. They were upset that their only daughter had married beneath her. They tried their best for me, too, but my father won in the end." A host of suppressed memories now unfolded. Father reenlisted in the Army. Mother and daughter felt bereft, but this time, instead of trying to make do on his meager soldier's salary, mother took a job. While she worked, Donna was left in the care of the grandparents. Mrs. Hutchcomb remembered those years with pleasure. Grandma was a wonderful cook and looked after the little girl with great care.

There were a few incidents that puzzled her even as a child, and she now brought her puzzlement into the sessions. She was never allowed to play with other children. When she invited some of them into her grandparents' spacious yard, grandmother immediately sent them away again. She was also in the habit of locking Donna up in her bedroom when she went to church. Donna at first didn't mind because Grandma left her supplied with cookies and milk and many toys, but after a while she rebelled. She complained to her mother who insisted that she follow Grandma's rules. Mother tried to explain that Grandmother was of a different religion than they and had to go to church very often. Catholics went every day and twice on Sundays, it seemed. Donna was intrigued. Could she be a Catholic too? No way, mother shrieked. She had become a Protestant upon marrying father, and Donna was not to upset anyone by having foolish thoughts about adopting another religion.

The mode in which Mrs. Hutchcomb brought this part of her life into the analysis was extraordinarily disjointed. There was little continuity over the hours, almost as though we were just beginning an analysis. She was aware of this and explained to me that "it is like I'm seeing sunlit flashes and pictures and then I tell you about them. But they only last a second, like fractured images. When they disappear, I tell you something else."

Interwoven with reminiscences about her life with her grandparents were obsessive expressions of regret that Matt was no longer available to her. Recently, she had been in touch with his mother "in order to be near him." She used the image of her youthful love for Matt as a device to calm herself. When something in the fragments of her memory about her grandparents bothered her, she would switch to images of Matt and how they had loved each other. Their romance constituted a form of personal myth (Kris, 1956) and became the refuge for resistance to remembering and working-through. I conceptualized her use of Matts image as a defense against the transference, but she would have none of that. She felt that my interpretations along those lines "spoiled her youthful innocence." She then drew a picture of herself as incredibly trusting and naive, unable to defend herself against a world full of evil because she was so trusting.

It became clear that Mrs. Hutchcomb's romantic fantasies were not only a defense against memories of trauma during the oedipal phase. Her personal myth included traces of much earlier developmental phases, leading me to believe that her distortions would be particularly tenacious and difficult to analyze. As we worked to understand her belief system, Mrs. Hutchcomb again began to complain about her husband's inability to please her sexually and fervently wished to meet Matt "to finish what we started and never accomplished." She was furious that Matt had children by someone else. Her fury gathered even greater strength when her mother let it slip that father also had a child by "that woman" who had brought so much unhappiness into their family life. Mrs. Hutchcomb had no interest in finding out more about her phantom sibling. She thought her mother had lied and insisted that her mother often distorted the truth knowingly in order to manipulate her family. The heretofore idealized, angelic image of the mother now shifted to a vision of a controlling, selfish, and ignorant virago.

Concomitantly, Mrs. Hutchcomb's imagery now shifted toward children in all sorts of predicaments. The tightness and pain in her jaw, which had temporarily abated, returned. Dissociation once again became part and parcel of every session. But this time she was able to describe images when she returned from these "absences." On occasion, she thought she had slept and dreamed in my presence. The images were always of children in trouble, in particular of children who set fires. One of the "dreams" she reported during one of these sessions also contained children and fire. In it she had a Korean godchild who was being taken care of by a wild man who resembled her grandfather. The child played with matches, which she quickly swallowed when the grandfather appeared. Mrs. Hutchcomb saw that the child was in danger and went to look for her father, who was too busy to pay attention. She then went to get help from her mother, but mother was suffering from a sunburn and required her to put lotion on her burning back. When she administered the lotion, her own hand began to burn. Large rats appeared and carried fire everywhere.

Mrs. Hutchcomb found it difficult to leave the session after this dream. She was certain that it meant more than any other dream she had ever had and was angry with me for not interpreting anything without her associations. She begged me over and over again to tell her what it meant, as though I held her very life in my hands. She complained of feeling naked and without any protection and certain that she could not associate. Nothing reminded her of anything. After several agonizing hours, she sat up and looked at me wildly. "I know what happened," she declared. She lay down again and in the most orderly fashion began to tell me why she had not been allowed to play with other children and why her grandmother had locked her into her room when grandma had to absent herself.

"Grandfather was overly fond of watching me on the potty. They had a big old house with those big wooden toilet seats with brass pulleys. I would have fallen in, so they had a potty for me. He always came running when I had to sit on it and told me what a pretty little duff I had. I didn't know what he meant, my front or my back. He cleaned me off with a lot of paper or, when we had the time, he used a lot of soapy water. He put perfume and bath oil in it. I thought it was like the Baby Jesus when the three wise men brought frankincense and myrrh. When he cleaned me, he stuck his finger in my behind. At first I cried, but then I liked it. He always told me I had a good little duff, very rosy and pink. When grandma found out, she cried and tried to beat him up, but of course he was much stronger than she. She yelled and said, 'Now you want to destroy Donna like you destroyed your own daughter.' "

Mrs. Hutchcomb declared that on some level she had known all along why she was kept away from other children. "It was to keep grandpa away from children, not me. And she locked me in to save me." As a child, she had blamed herself for having such a round, pink duff and hoped she could make it brown and dirty so that grandpa wouldn't "clean her." On the other hand. she found his ministrations a good deal more exciting than when grandma took care of her. Grandma even made her clean herself, and she resented that a lot.

What shocked Mrs. Hutchcomb more than her own fate was that her mother had been molested in the same way. "It is simply not possible," she repeated. "It could not happen in such a family as ours. We are all religious in our own way. How could grandpa have done such a thing? And if he did that to my mother, doesn't that make my mother my sister? Do you think I should confront her? "Anger at her beloved grandmother surfaced strongly. She professed to understand why the old lady had been abandoned to strangers when she became senile and was eventually "put away" rather than nursed at home. After all, grandma had defended grandpa and had not been able to stop his behavior. She simply kept children away from him. "But why not me? Why did she not keep him from me?"

Mrs. Hutchcomb embraced her victimization. She asked herself why her mother had left her with a man she knew to be a child molester and came to the conclusion that mother "wanted me to know what she had been through so that I would be a better daughter." The many times when she had slept in her mother's bed came back to haunt her. She seemed to recall that mother had asked her to suck on her breasts, but she pushed that thought away. She thought of confronting her mother but gave up that thought because she was certain that mother would deny everything. More dreams surfaced in which a child played with fire, or was consumed by fire, or was hunted down by huge burning rats. The rats spread the fire.

Barely able to contain her rage, Mrs. Hutchcomb at first wanted to avenge herself, though it was not clear on what or whom she wanted to vent her hatred. Often enough she turned on me to accuse me of putting things into her head that hadn't been there before, or at the very least lowering the walls that had fenced in her memories. Analysis had definitely added to her suffering, she claimed. She yearned for a way to relieve herself of the steady internal pressure that made her doubt her own perceptions and memories. She tried to deny that the "shudders" she had experienced as a child were now again in evidence. She even shuddered on the couch with open pleasure but then asked me if she had experienced anything at all. Clearly, she had to ignore her reawakened sensory pleasure and terror in connection with being anally penetrated by grandfather's finger. All other physical symptoms, however, such as the headaches and the pain in her jaw, had disappeared without their exact meaning being analyzed.

"For want of anybody else," as Mrs. Hutchcomb put it, she turned for relief to her husband and was surprised at the "ecstasy and passion" that entered her lovemaking. Unfortunately, Mr. Hutchcomb was frightened by so much ardor and begged his wife to pray with him for their mutual enlightenment as to what this "lustful contamination" might mean. Again, Mrs. Hutchcomb quite openly stated that she thought it was the analysis "and poking into every little hole" that overstimulated her. A mutative interpretation (Strachey, 1934) that she felt my words penetrating her like grandfather's finger brought her some relief and enabled her to become active in the reconstruction of what happened between her and her mother.

As she understood that my words were not grandfather's finger, she was also able to understand that it was not she who had nursed inappropriately on her mother's breast when she was already of latency age. It was her mother who had "tweaked her nipples and kissed her bottom." Mrs. Hutchcomb literally writhed on the couch when she recalled somatically, but not at first mentally, how her mother had stimulated her. I did not try to clarify anything at this stage but instead became the witness to the tragedy of Mrs. Hutchcomb's early life. Gradually, she was able to disidentify from the abusive internalized mother image. Eventually, she was able to confide in a good friend at her office who, far from rejecting her or making her feel ashamed, suggested she join a group of adult incest survivors. Much encouraged at such a positive response from the first real friend she had made since her girlhood, Mrs. Hutchcomb went to one meeting and came back horrified. "They don't try to work out anything at all," she told me. "They just sit around and complain." Nonetheless, this bit of reality testing gave her enough courage to slowly connect her physical sensations with what had happened between her and her mother. That unhappy woman had kissed and fondled her daughter's vagina until the little girl "shuddered." Simultaneously, she told the child that this was all right, that because they were mother and daughter they could kiss and fondle each other "all over" but that this would be their secret and make them best friends forever.

The interpretation that mother had turned her own passively endured seduction into an active experience by using her child's body for relief made sense to Mrs. Hutchcomb. But she still needed further proof. She tried to coerce me into validating as real any fantasy that came into her head and tried repeatedly to test me by threatening to end the analysis prematurely. She had developed a self-protective kind of intuition that allowed her to pick up minute clues in my, and other's behavior. For instance, she was quite right in assuming that I expected her not to finish her analysis. I had come to this temporary conclusion because it seemed to me that although Mrs. Hutchcomb had introjected my thinking and cognitive style and, to a certain extent, had separated from the malignant maternal image, she still had not sufficiently cathected, or built, a positive self-image. Despite the fact that she was now rapidly advancing in her work situation and had become the supervisor of an office staffed with 20 people, she still comported herself like the junior executive I had met four years before. The additional money she earned was deposited with an investment firm so that her savings soon outpaced those of her husband. This was no source of pride to her. She did not change her modest way of life or her relationship with her husband. It took two years before she was able to integrate her own perceptions, feelings, fantasies, and memories sufficiently to decide that she was not "mad as a hatter." Almost ready to end the analysis without traversing a separation period, Mrs. Hutchcomb decided to look for proof of her seduction instead. She once again became impervious to interpretation. Euphoria reigned as she set out to "confront and conquer."

I feel as though she were literally trying to make me into the finger up her cute little duff. My own narcissistic needs are clamoring when she decides to relegate me to an archaic part object in the service of becoming a sort of psychological soothing function to her. All she wants, once again, is for me to mirror, mirror, mirror. Apparently much less restructuring of her psyche has taken place than I had hoped for. It occurs to me that I have no nickname for Mrs. H. as I have for all the others. Funny, how old Barchilon's little "trick" of nicknaming patients to begin reading one's countertransference has stayed with me! But Mrs. H. always appears to me as what she pretends to be, namely, Mrs. Hutchcomb. That's it. She is a pretender to the state of womanhood. It's all that pretentious pretending about the differing classes of society that makes my hackles—and my projected finger-anal-penis?—rise. All that stuff I am reading about countertransference being something like the patient's allowing the analyst to project her observing ego into their internal spaces absolutely makes me furious!!!

What patients like Mrs. H. the Pretender do is to intrude into my internal spaces, and with such vigor that I feel like avenging myself for being made into a masturbating finger. Thank God, no, thank my dear old analyst that I can admit this stuff and so stay functioning as an analyst. Maybe those intellectual types can't allow themselves to feel much. Anyway, they are of use in letting me divert my fury from Mrs. H. onto them. When I make contact with her; no-contact is a euphemism. In her case, I am swept over by chaos, not even rage, which, after all, is an entity. Her inner life is chaos, still, after all this time. No differentiation between self and the malignant part objects whom I seem to have joined inside of her. What to do?

Maybe my own fury is sparked by disappointment that, after I've worked so hard for so long, so little structure has grown . . . . Yes, indeed, the analyst's narcissistic needs can be great!! Poor Mrs. Hutchcomb the Pretender. Are we both pretending? Maybe I just overestimated her developmental level. After all, why should she believe what she discovered on my couch? There are few enough trustworthy people in her life, with Matt the distant, somewhat delusional lover being the steadiest and most nurturing! Maybe finding the reality factors will shore her up.

THE SEARCH FOR HISTORIC TRUTH

Mrs. Hutchcomb became a faithful reporter of her efforts to find people who could corroborate the story of her life. However, she seemed to need and want only my cognitive attention, carefully negating any transference interpretation. An alter-ego transference (Kohut, 1971) had been ushered in by the activation of her grandiose self. She once again had to deny my importance to her and her dependency on me. I saw this denial as a defense against possibly feeling as much hatred and narcissistic rage at me as she had felt against her mother and father and grandparents. By thus devaluing me as too weak to withstand her affects, she simultaneously protected her shaky internalizations of aspects of me and the analytic process, which she acknowledged to be helpful.

Mrs. Hutchcomb was sure she could and would conquer all obstacles in her quest for proof of incest. She became quite an ingenious detective, demonstrating the reawakening of a sharp intelligence. For instance, something about her birth certificate and her parents' anniversary date had long troubled her. Comparing the dates consciously for the first time, she realized that she "must have been conceived out of wedlock." She responded to this finding with despair, feeling herself to be narcissistically wounded. She speculated that "being the offspring of an illicit affair," she would be little regarded by her mother since her very presence would be a reminder of mother's transgression. But instead of pouting and withdrawing, she decided to contact the physician who had assisted at her birth and whose name was listed on her birth certificate. He turned out to be someone whom she had known for a long time, a physician who had taken care of most of the families in her part of the town. He had long since retired and seemed glad when she contacted him for an appointment. He thought she wanted to chat and have tea and talk about old times. He was shocked by her questions and told her to "let sleeping dogs lie." Enraged, she demanded to know what he meant by that. She badgered the old gentleman until he was willing to reveal that her mother had fled to him as a teenager to protest her mistreatment by her father. He had concluded after examination that she had indeed been penetrated. He had refused, however, to believe her allegations that she been sexually abused by her father and summoned Mrs. Hutchcomb's grandmother to take her daughter home. He had strongly recommended that the distraught young girl be married off soon. He had felt that "a regulated sexual life" such as marriage is supposed to offer would cure what he thought of as the hysterical fantasies of a prematurely developed young girl. He beseeched Mrs. Hutchcomb not let anyone know of his disclosures, which he apparently regretted as soon as he made them. But Mrs. Hutchcomb dismissed him as "a senile fool." She had no sympathy for the old gentleman but felt glee at having been able "to make him putty in my hands." She was certain that he had given her enough evidence of her grandfather's incestuous behavior but "nothing that would stand up to the court of her own conscience."

There was a compulsive quality about her undertaking that I could not interpretively touch. Although there were strong elements of self-healing in Mrs. Hutchcomb's quest, her actions also revealed that she still was not able to trust her own perceptions sufficiently to believe them or begin to build more separate self- and object-representations. It seemed of greater importance to her to build a guiltless mother image than to heal herself. Identification with the aggressor was so strong that she kept stressing her mother's great beauty and the horrible nightmare her childhood must have been. Mother's sad fate was mourned, but not her own. It was as though she had made herself into the rescuer of her mother. She did not permit analytic investigation of the implications of this swing to the negative oedipal conflict. When I gingerly touched on the subject of an adult daughter and her mother being so inter-twined as to have the wish to rescue each other, Mrs. Hutchcomb hotly accused me of being an apologist for homosexuality. My silence seemed to her to confirm her suspicion. At the same time, a dream in which a snake came out of a box frightened her. She thought that I had forced my ideas into her. Rather than allowing examination of inceasingly erotized aspects of the transference, Mrs. Hutchcomb speculated, correctly, as it turned out, that, to escape her incestuous home, her mother had allowed herself to become pregnant with the first young man who made himself available to her. Now mother seemed even more courageous to Mrs. Hutchcomb. After all, she her-self had been spared the dreadful burden of an illegitimate child owing to her mother's intervention, or so she claimed. Her mother, not she, was seen as the victim and was idealized.

Nevertheless, her search continued. I was given a blow-by-blow recounting of who had said what in regard to her detec-tive work. By now, she had involved a number of her family members and old friends, without disclosing the reason for her inquiries. She had at first made attempts to communicate her true intent but was stopped short by either their disbelief or the same advice the doctor had given her—to let well enough alone. But contact with older family members put her on the trail of a branch of the family she had not seen or heard from since childhood. Grandfather had been married before and was said to have other children. Mrs. Hutchcomb tracked down an elderly aunt who fully corroborated her story. The aunt had fled the household when she was 20 after seeing her father act in "a forbidden way with the new baby." Her flight had been seen as jealousy toward the second wife, Mrs. Hutchcomb's grandmother. Now in her 80s, the old lady seemed both delighted and relieved to have her niece appear out of nowhere.

But finding herself to be "right" did not prove to be the pana-cea Mrs. Hutchcomb had hoped for. Instead, she once again became depressed. The visits with her parents, which had ceased during her quest, now resumed. She haltingly ques-tioned her mother, who flew into a storm of outrage at being confronted with her daughter's question as to her "illicit" con-ception. "If I want to have a relationship with her, it'll have to be on her terms," Mrs. Hutchcomb correctly concluded. The illusion of a gallantly suffering mother-as-victim she had so laboriously constructed was shattered in an instant. Once again, Mrs. Hutchcomb found herself "let down and deserted by those who should love me but only make believe that I mean anything to them."

Turning to her husband, she found him to be securely ensconced as a deacon of his church. He felt calm and effective in the community, buoyed by his certainty that he was doing the work of God. He invited her to join him, in particular, in accepting "regulated marital relations in Christ." The offer to participate in the work of God rather than in mere psychoanalysis proved to be irresistible. Mrs. Hutchcomb said that she felt protected both by her husband and by his God. She became tearful when I interpreted that she possibly felt unprotected by me in her journey toward self-knowledge. Once again she shifted about on the couch, pulled down her skirt, made sure all the buttons on her blouse were closed. While I was considering whether or not to comment on her nonverbal behavior, she told me that she "did not feel uncomfortable talking about what happened with her grandfather. She felt uncomfortable only because she was "no longer connected to her mother." She realized that she was sorely needed by her mother to shore up the older woman's precarious sense of self. Simultaneously, once again reversing roles with her mother—nurturing her mother rather than being nurtured by her—allowed her to shift away from a transference that was rapidly becoming more and more sexualized.

Mrs. Hutchcomb was able to recognize that there had been pleasurable parts of her interactions with her grandfather, that it was enormously exciting to be locked in by grandmother and then have grandfather surreptitiously open the door with a wrench so that they could be together. She was desperately ashamed of this pleasure and angry that her mother must have felt similar pleasure. But once she had acknowledged that her mother might have felt pleasure as well as terror in regard to the same man, Mrs. Hutchcomb almost visibly pulled herself away from further self-examination. Competition and oedipal rivalry with mother were too dangerous. She made a conscious, verbalized choice "to conform. All this other stuff is too esoteric for me." Rather than continuing to search for her self and undergo further painful mourning in the possible restructuring of her psyche, Mrs. Hutchcomb abruptly ended the analysis. But she could not resist one more dramatic act: she sent me a second basket of roses with a thank you card.

DISCUSSION

At the end of Mrs. Hutchcomb's analysis it was not clear just what her unresolved transference situation might be. I suspect that in the hidden recesses of her mind I remained the maternal seductress, the penetrating grandfather, and the idealized Matt all rolled into one uncomfortable and semidelusional imago despite efforts on both of our parts to resolve this dilemma through interpretation. To allow conscious examination of these transference constellations was too frightening for Mrs. Hutchcomb, perhaps rightly so. Permitting herself to see me as someone who could be trusted, might have evoked even more frightening and fragmenting regressions. She had already lost the idealized version of her mother. Now she feared isolation and the total loss of her reality ego. A submissive merger with the all-powerful God of her husband seemed preferable. She used external conformity as a defense against fragmentation and regression.

Although gains had been made in that she was symptom free and no longer had to resort to body language, her object- and self-representations remained primitive. Her object representations at times seemed willfully delusional, that is, she behaved as though she knew that her assessment of herself and others was incorrect but wanted it to be that way. (I am using this laborious description in order to avoid the more familiar term "omnipotence.") Mrs. Hutchcomb experienced herself as totally helpless, a plaything of fate. At the same time she was convinced that she could turn around, or shape to her liking, the secrets of her family's past. In the unresolved transference, she sorely needed to deny my existence as an independent other and reduced me to a function, rather than an individuated human presence in her internal world. Even given this circumstance, those internalizations helped to alleviate some of her pain. For instance, although she had not been able to integrate all she had discovered, she was able to include some measure of it in her thinking and feeling. Her formidable intellect became more useful to her. She was able to use its cognitive and reasoning aspects but did not permit herself to take the next step and connect it to libidinal and creative uses. Her intuition stayed in the service of self-protection and did not function to make contact with others. Her narcissistic preoccupation remained the search for an omnipotent rescuer who could magically heal all wounds. Denial stayed in the foreground and at times blocked her reality perception, a state of affairs that has grave consequences that have been brilliantly depicted by Dorpat (1983). He hypothesizes that there are four phases present when denial is used as a defense: (1) preconscious appraisal of danger, (2) painful affect, (3) cognitive arrest, and (4) screen behavior (pp. 56–57).

After Mrs. Hutchcomb had gained some foothold in the world of human interaction, that is, after she had internalized some mirroring as growth-producing and grudgingly accepted me as a selfobject, she created an inner world of youthful romance that at first served her well. Merged with idealized figures like Matt and an improbably omniscient analyst, she set out to construct a self. But there were too many obstacles. A totally unempathic object world still surrounded her and would not respond to her even when she resorted to acting out and rebellion. But her rebellion did no good. Those around her remained unaffected. Her husband turned even farther away from her, and her mother proved unequal to confrontation. There was nothing left for her but to deny that which was already about to bloom, namely, self-cohesion. Rather than deal with the more painful affect she unconsciously knew would arise if she allowed the perceived danger—accepting her temporary dependence on her analyst and the analytic process—to enter her consciousness, she settled for more denial and focused instead on the reality of her incest trauma. But she paid a high price for this shifted focus. When she no longer thought about the consequences of her trauma and its many derivatives, her cognition became less sharp. As Dorpat (1983) puts it,

in the cognitive arrest phase the subject in fantasy unconsciously attacks the concrete representation of whatever he considers to be the cause of his psychic pain. The fantasy attempts to destroy the painful object and arrest the subjects' thinking at a primary process level. The fantasy attack on the painful object and the consequent cognitive arrest is followed by screen behavior. Screen behavior is defined as the ideas, fantasies, affects, and overt behaviors motivated by the need to fill in the gaps created by the cognitive arrest, to substitute a different object relation for the one subjectively lost and to support the defensive aims of the preceding phase [p. 57].

Mrs. Hutchcomb's mother failed to grasp empathically her daughter's attempt to construct a new relationship between them. So did her husband. This double disappointment in the real world accentuated the narcissistic disappointment suffered in the analysis when I turned out to be anything but omniscient. She experienced both my silences and my interpretations as unbearable intrusions, although she admitted that some of them were helpful to her. For instance, when she felt drowsy and dissociated, she regularly, directly afterward, reported feeling calm and relaxed. Yet in retrospect she felt spied on and was angry when together we discovered that during these sleeplike absences she had relived aspects of the incestuous relationships with both her mother and her grandfather. She had to deny that such a replay of past events on my couch in my office was unconsciously intended in some way to involve me, either as the abuser or as the victim. Her need to keep me at arm's length heralded fear that she would repeat with me what had occurred between her and her abusers. She needed to run away from such a dire eventuality. Nonetheless, I wonder if Mrs. Hutchcomb's gift of roses did not, among other less constructive aspects, also symbolize acknowledgement that she had made some gains in the analytic interaction.

SUMMARY

On a phenomenologic basis, Mrs. Raphael's and Mrs. Hutchcomb's case histories have similarities. Both women at the beginning of treatment were confused and unable cognitively to understand the complicated dynamics of their families. They used denial as a favorite defense. Body language, somatic memories, and the need to act instead of remembering was common to both. Each had constructed a narrative of her life that acted as an outward structure to explain and enable her to tolerate the strange interactions within her dysfunctional family. These narratives sounded so smooth yet improbable that at first I tended to see them as a form of pseudologia. But neither Mrs. Raphael nor Mrs. Hutchcomb was lying. They were both convinced of the truth of their personal myths. Identification with the aggressor and dissociation were defenses they shared, especially dissociation as enactment of trauma. Both women were overcome by obsessive doubts when they analytically uncovered the depth of their incestuous traumas. But there, in my opinion, the similarities end.

The material Mrs. Raphael uncovered shored up her ego and helped her to make changes. She even managed to view her hapless mother as pitiable and was able to acknowledge that the woman must have fallen prey to psychotic fragmentation in the absence of her husband and then used her young daughter to quiet rampant drives. Mrs. Raphael saw as tragic the circumstance of her aunt/sister's conception and life and wished she could have helped the dead woman. She regretted deeply the necessity of staying away from her mother until she herself could judge how much exposure to the older woman's dictatorial wishes she could safely "take" without resorting to withdrawal as a defense against the invasion of her body boundaries. But Mrs. Raphael, by the time she went on her fact-finding mission, already believed in the truth of what she had uncovered. She was able to read correctly her body signals and "loved the freedom from confusion" that followed the painful process of remembering. Even in the beginning phase of treatment, when she was still compelled to act rather than to speak on the couch, she was able to take in aspects of offered interpretations and bear the weight of transferences. I believe this ability to trust—if only on a very fleeting and unreliable basis—must have come about because Mrs. Raphael always "knew" that her mother was odd. From an early age she understood the family at large to be protective of her person against her mother. Therefore, her perception of reality was not as distorted as was that of Mrs. Hutchcomb. The sometimes chaotic dynamics of Mrs. Raphael's clan allowed her to keep possibilities open and view her own life with a smidgen of hope even when she was most deprived. In her words: "I always knew there was another world out there that is not so crazy."

In contrast, Mrs. Hutchcomb's family, especially her mother, was "always right." In order to bind her painful overstimulation and to survive psychologically, she had to become as rigid and inflexible as her immediate family. Forever in search of an omni-

potent rescuer, she had become isolated, fearful, and rigid herself. When the painful stiffness of her jaw was analyzed and
revealed itself to be a displacement upward, she thought she
had found an omnipotent rescuer in me, her analyst. Disappointment followed. What she discovered in her search for the
truth was too frightening to be integrated. Two abusers, her
grandfather and her mother, had warped her development too
severely. Perhaps also because the same man had abused both
her mother and her, she could not free herself from her mother
as a fellow victim. She went so far as to claim that she had sexually used her mother, not the other way around. This was not
only an identification with the aggressor, but also a genuine
effort to help her mother, whom she saw as more fragile and
damaged than herself. To keep psychologically growing at all,
she identified with the rigid structure and demands for obedi-
ence and conformity her family exacted. Although she intellectually accepted that her somatic remembering had foreshad-
owed the memories that were substantiated by her exhaustive
and exhausting research into the past, she could not really bring
herself to integrate what she knew. She could not forgive her
mother. But she could not lose her either. Her compromise was
to accept "things as they were" and to slip silently back into the
mold made for her. She repeated this compromise with her
husband.

In both analyses, my countertransference was of great
importance. Dealing with how I felt included permitting myself
to regress during free association outside of the sessions. More
than once I caught myself in the wish to be more supportive
than I believed necessary for the continued growth of my patients. There were many struggles between my work ego and
my libidinal responses to both women. I don't believe I could
have stayed emotionally open to Mrs. Hutchcomb, for instance,
if I had not caught myself intellectualizing in order to ward off
anger. Often I seemed to understand more about her objects
than about her as though even in the analysis they were more
important than she. To keep the focus and the emotional emphasis on her was not always easy because she herself slipped
away so often. When she left, I must admit to regretting that
we could not conclude our work together. I wondered if it would
have been appropriate to have been more supportive and to
abandon my belief that Mrs. Hutchcomb was capable of the

hard work of analysis. The question was: Would she have stayed in analysis if I had changed my technique? Possibly. However, I believe that if she had stayed on owing to a change of therapeutic stance, her inner structure would not have changed further given her erotized transference. That is, she would likely have experienced a different treatment approach as a further seduction.

This was not so with Mrs. Raphael. Although she was often difficult and her volatile mood swings hard to keep up with, our good working alliance and her willingness to "look life in the eye" proved beneficial to both of us. I learned a good deal about my particular analytic instrument by working with her. Trusting my own signals and recognizing the shifts of my imagery was a gift she left me with.

Reflecting on the work with both these women, I am once again struck by how love-starved children manage to find a kindness here and a bit of warmth there, just enough to keep them alive and growing. For instance, Mrs. Hutchcomb's grandmother, by protecting her and providing her with a warm atmosphere, also helped her to keep a sense of self-cohesion and very rudimentary self-respect. Mrs. Hutchcomb knew, even as a little girl, that her grandfather was not the kind man he pretended to be. She was able to accept her mother's guidance as a form of love even though she recognized that she was being controlled and manipulated into a masochistic kind of surrender. And, strange as it may seem, she was prized by her family as the one offspring "who had done well." This tiny bit of acclaim sustained her, making her into the champion of the idealized, victimized mother.

That Mrs. Raphael's mother loved her and simultaneously abused her was also clear. During her more quiet times, the mother would tell Mrs. Raphael what a splendid little girl she had been and how helpful around the house. Even now, she was proud of her daughter and granddaughter. Mrs. Raphael thought "that mother seems to think she lives only for me. Maybe that's to make up for the terrible things that happened to both of us."

Although the analytic data concerning the incestuous mothers necessarily remain incomplete even though the daughters so thoroughly researched the past, I hypothesize that both of these women's inner lives were undifferentiated. Their fluid body boundaries did not always permit them to see their children as separate from themselves. Therefore, they simply used the bodies of their daughters to empty themselves of overwhelming sexual tension. In this overstepping of generational and individual boundaries, they appear to have followed the example of their fathers. They knew only superficially that what they were doing was wrong. Their life experience had taught them that they could do as they wished. But, at the same time, they knew that they had to conform to society's rules somehow if they were to stay accepted and accept themselves as well. Therefore, they simply passed the burden of shame and guilt on to their children by confusing them with the message that they could do forbidden things with each other, provided nobody, not even their little victims, acknowledged it.

These two mothers seem to have shared a selectively punitive superego that allowed them to suppress with a vengeance their children's aggression. They had to stay outwardly pliable and conform. I also have the impression that they were not clear about their own sexual identity. It seemed to be unimportant to them that they acted out their own dramas with little females who, in their fantasies, must have temporarily symbolized themselves while they acted the part of the penetrating father.

Mahler (1971) conceptualizes the inability of the child to own her body:

> If there was a major failure of integration during the first three subphases of separation-individuation, particularly on the level of gender identity, the child might not have taken autonomous, representationally clearly separated possession of his or her own bodily self . . . such male and female patients alike will ever so often act out in the transference and in life . . . the unconscious role of a cherished or rejected part of the parents' hypothetical body-self ideal [pp. 416–417].

While such developmental constructs are extremely helpful in explaining phenomena, the clinical situation is not quite so structured, nor do I think along these developmental lines when analyzing. I have found it helpful to disengage my thinking from phase specificity during treatment and to turn to the use of metaphor instead. The key issues for the patients I have just described were autonomy versus control, conformity versus individuality. Their transference situations clearly expressed these conflicts. The patterns of their lives had been distorted so early that these issues of autonomy versus control, conformity versus individuality, were present on all developmental levels we encountered. According to Stern (1985), there is always an earlier edition of conflict

> that either cannot be retrieved because of repression or cannot be recognized because of distortions or transformations between the primary and later editions . . . . it is not always the case, however, and even if it were, the unmasked earliest edition is rarely where theory predicts its origin point should be [pp. 261–262].

Perhaps it is not necessary to retrieve the earliest version of conflict, merely the most destructive one. Certainly this seems to have been so in the cases of Mrs. Raphael and Mrs. Hutchcomb. When inner and outer worlds become as entangled and enmeshed as they were for these two women, perhaps that is the only possible path.

Chapter 4
Mother–Son Incest

I n the previous chapters the subject was maternal incest also.
Two mothers not only passed on their own passively experienced incestuous traumas to their children, they also acted
as though they preferred to penetrate their daughters with their
forefingers and to masturbate them in a fantasized reenact-
ment of being penetrated by their fathers. Mrs. Hutchcomb's
mother in addition required her daughter to nurse on her breast
long after that was age appropriate. Both young women nevertheless had a firmly established core gender identity (Stoller,
1985). Yet they had doubts about the functions of their femaleness and did not achieve object-related orgasm until they managed to distance themselves from both the actual, frightening,
demanding, needy mother and the internalized devouring
mother imago. Both women at times were confused about who
their love objects could be. Mrs. Raphael actually tried to act
in an apparently homosexual way. Both women felt drawn to
female friends to provide maternal care they had been denied.
But because of their traumas they erotized these friendly feelings and then became frightened by their own tender sensuality (Siegel, 1994).

Although I understood these phenomena as manifestations
of an eroticized maternal transference (Wrye and Welles, 1989),
neither of the women exhibited the blank and insistent
demandingness sometimes seen in women who during psychoanalytic treatment need to complete their insufficiently
cathected body image (Siegel, 1984, 1988). Mrs. Raphael and
Mrs. Hutchcomb managed to traverse their developmental
phases more completely than do women whose body images
were defective. I hypothesize that the premature use of their
genital apparatus by the at times highly erotic and physically
tender ministrations of their mothers permitted the cathexis

of their physiologic femaleness, though at the price of distorting some of their ego functions. This is in contrast to other women whom I have treated who had unempathic mothers. For them, lack of empathy and disregard by narcissistic mothers precluded the formation of a healthy body image. In Mrs. Raphael and Mrs. Hutchcomb, the body images appeared to be complete though at times labile.

Bernstein (1990) comments that women who have been incestuously abused have not been reported to develop the common fantasies of oedipal victors, such as males who have been their mothers' lovers (Shengold, 1980). These fantasies include a feeling of invincibility, of being "king of the world." I speculate that, on the contrary, being mother's sexual plaything did nothing to inflate Mrs. Hutchcomb's or Mrs. Raphael's narcissism. Rather, they felt leeched of all libidinal supplies and were confused about who was supposed to nurture whom. In some of their fantasies and dreams they revealed that they saw themselves as passively female and their mothers as penetratingly male. The homosexual aspects of their mother–daughter relationships were at first denied but acted out with female friends.

But the two young men whose cases I recount in this chapter do not fit the description of oedipal victors either. Perhaps this has to do with the fact that other reports about mother–son incest dealt with adolescents or young men who had not repressed the incestuous events (Shengold, 1980; Margolis, 1984). The brief characterologic description of Gabbard and Twemlow's (1994) patient who remembered incest in the third year of his analysis is closer to my own clinical experience. Although they speculate that their patient's life experience might have contributed to the formation of a hypervigilant kind of narcissistic personality disorder, they place emphasis on the expectation of humiliation, punishment, and abandonment in the object relationships of such men.

Val Brewster and Simon Avital expected to be misused and mistreated as well. But they did not report having committed incest with their mothers until the treatment process was well established. Val Brewster one day simply started talking about it as though he had always remembered it but had merely "forgotten" to report it. Yet his "remembering to report" followed the interpretation of a significant dream. Both men feared castration by their mothers and rescued themselves from such dire threats by resorting to homosexual fantasies, some homosexual acts, and the repeatedly voiced wish that they could become entirely homosexual. Nevertheless, neither man ever permitted himself a full homosexual relationship, even ran away from it when it became a possibility. Neither one of them was subject to dissociation. Both were rather flamboyant in their appearance and fanatic about their health. I saw in these attempts at "looking good and feeling good," as Simon Avital put it, strivings to mother themselves. These self-nurturing gestures could be seen as vestiges of omnipotence. But many hypochondriacal preoccupations were also present, leading me to hypothesize a failed omnipotence and insufficient resolution of the rapprochement phase instead. At the beginning of treatment, both men were aware that their mothers and their families were dysfunctional and vociferously condemned what they saw as inappropriate behavior. Perhaps this ability to judge their mothers' behavior realistically can be understood as part of the oedipal victor's triumph.

VAL BREWSTER

Two telephone calls, one from his former analyst and one from his mother, acquainted me with parts of Val Brewster's history. His previous analyst had been forced by circumstances to retire before he intended to. He asked me if I would take on Val, who, he felt, should be with a female analyst. Somewhat taken aback by the request for a female analyst from a colleague known for his orthodoxy, I agreed to see Val Brewster for a consultation. Almost immediately after that call, Mrs. Brewster phoned and asked for an appointment for her son. I asked that he call himself and found myself under fire. Mrs. Brewster felt that because she and her husband were financing their son's therapy, they were entitled to a running progress report. Certain that she had not received such reports from my colleague, I told her that I was not prepared to take on her son under those circumstances. Mrs. Brewster immediately apologized and promised to have her son call. He did call that same evening. I was not at all sure that an analysis would be possible given this beginning.

But then I met young Mr. Brewster. He arrived punctually, clad in trendy sportswear, his whole person an advertisement for physical fitness. He assumed that we would follow the format he had become acquainted with during his previous treatment. He politely gave me his address and told me that he had just finished an internship in his profession and was now waiting for one of several prospective jobs to materialize. He professed wanting to work "hard in the analysis so that he wouldn't screw up whatever job he got." When he judged that he had given enough information of this sort, he lay down on the couch in a most matter-of-fact way. He had been well trained in the rules of analysis. He told me what he thought I should know about him and what he and his previous analyst had worked on. He was known to be stubborn, and he and his analyst had decided that this was a trait that held him back. He told an anecdote about himself that sounded well rehearsed. When he was two or three years old, his father asked him to empty an ashtray. When he did not obey, the father beat him and he still wouldn't do it. His mother had to intervene to make peace. In the end, he did not empty the ashtray but apologized for not doing so.

Apparently Val Brewster used this highly condensed screen memory as a guide for understanding his stubbornness. He felt he was also stubborn about "this thing with girls." He wanted to get married, or at least go steady with a girl, but could not bring himself to ask a girl to go out with him. Twenty-six years old, he was still a virgin and was sure that his friends laughed at him behind his back over it. He had tried many times to have a girlfriend but had always failed because he was "too stubborn." He wanted to be married for "the prestige of it" and was even willing to "make believe we would get married", as long as a girl was willing to go out with him. Given his muscular, rather manly appearance, I found it hard to believe that he had difficulties meeting girls. No, he said, I had misunderstood. He did not have trouble meeting girls, just making love to them repulsed him. Girls found this out very soon and then wouldn't go out with him any more. Even though his mother had "coached" him before dates, things always went wrong. Sometimes he thought he was homosexual but "doing it with guys" also turned him off.

Each session, he revealed more about himself as though this were the easiest thing in the world to do. I watched for a sign that he missed his former analyst or that he mourned his loss. Finally, I asked him if he thought the sessions here were similar to those he had had before. For a moment, he was perplexed but then "reassured" me. According to him, it didn't matter who sat behind the couch as long as "they knew what they were doing." But my question did set off another train of thought.

While he was in the first year of his treatment with my predecessor, he had overcome his aversion to women long enough to seek out a "hooker." He asked her for fellatio but could maintain an erection only when thinking about his male friends and his male therapist. He found this encounter highly unsatisfactory because he was a "perfectionist." Something was missing in his interaction with the hooker. He supposed it was not knowing her name. But he purposely did not ask for it because then she would have had a right to know his name and would be able to find him afterwards. He had discussed this with his analyst, who wanted to know why he thought this woman would pursue him. Val Brewster was perplexed about this question to this day. His mother had always told him that "once a girl has her claws into you, she'll never let go. That's why you have to be careful." He had learned how to be a perfectionist from his mother, who had to work hard at it, given her temper. Mother had to learn to keep her temper with him not only because she became afraid when "he tensed his biceps at her," but because his therapist had told him to tell his mother that it would not help him to like women any better if she continually put him down.

I was still thinking of asking Mr. Brewster to sit up while doing therapy. I wondered if eye contact might not facilitate some sort of recognition in him that it did matter who was sitting behind the couch. I quickly realized that this was my desire to be seen by him as a person but that he, on the other hand, would have to develop a bit more before he could understand the concept of object constancy.

In almost every session there was a report of his mother's "trying to control her temper but failing." She was an excellent cook and housekeeper, he reported. His father was "thrilled with the way she handled clients he invited home when big contracts were about to be concluded." Val had to be on display also during such occasions and was often called on to escort the daughters, or even the wives, of his father's customers. He found these women "offensive and mean, out to get a man for all he's got." Of course, he readily admitted, he did not yet have much despite his appearance, which he judged to be good, and his health, which he knew to be excellent; but he had good prospects and found women's lack of interest in him humiliating. Finally, he confessed that just maybe he himself had something to do with their lack of interest. His real wish was to be able "to suck on his own penis if he could only bend down deep enough." He thought this wish was "a perversion, but at least it wasn't homosexual."

This fellow makes me sleepy. That flat drone is hypnotic. A child, really, despite all that paranoia. Wonder if Ma is psychotic? Where does so much sleepiness come from? Actually, I sometimes want to laugh at his naive assumptions. Must watch then. Narcissistic withdrawal from whom by whom? I remember a supervisory session with an early control analyst. I'm working my guts out to report on my analysand properly, and this guy falls asleep. I didn't even notice until I heard him snore. I idolized this person, I remember. I was petrified, hurt, didn't know what to do. Fortunately, he woke up right away and looked benignly at me, smiling his dimples at me. I asked if I had bored him. "No, my dear," he sonorously declaimed. "I was defending myself." He wouldn't discuss what he was defending himself against—my analysand, me, my reporting, or his own fantasies. Why in the world did I stay with him? So I've been on the other side of the falling asleep bit. What is Val Brewster telling me? Is he putting me to sleep—almost—because that way I can't attack like his mother? How does one engage such a person? Especially one who is so well trained from his previous analytic adventure. Must watch when and how he really connects.

The Midphase

I learned a lot about the happenings in this wealthy and well connected family during the first year of the analysis. Both Val and his sister, Janette, were held to tight budgets and constantly reminded of their good fortune in having wealthy parents. They each had to take interim jobs until they could become "properly situated." Val Brewster's future proper situation proved to be the topic of discussion for some time. He took a job in a children's psychiatric hospital while awaiting something more "meritorious" in another hospital. I tried to make him aware of the implications for his analysis if he should have to move away, but he was still convinced that "anyone would do" to sit behind the couch, though I saw it as progress that he returned to the subject often.

The pronounced paranoid flavor of earlier sessions gave way somewhat to a guarded friendliness in Mr. Brewster's accounts of how his sister made him angry because she dated his best friend and how he had bought himself a car telephone—then a very new and expensive toy—that was not part of any cellular network but allowed him to "look as though I am somebody." Of course he was unwilling or unable to discuss why his sister's dating his best friend made him angry or why he needed a toy phone to show off. I asked him to tell me what, in his opinion, constituted "being somebody." His answer was flat and emphatic: being somebody meant being married and having a meritorious job.

There still had been no reports of dreams or any sign that Mr. Brewster was capable of any but the most flat responsiveness. I was seriously contemplating a shift in technique, possibly trying a supportive, bridge-building approach, such as associating out loud about his material to show him how it is done (Lichtenberg, 1983). When I asked him whom he wished to contact with this car telephone, he laughed and said, "No one. It's just a game." But when I repeated that the use of such a toy must mean something, especially a toy that could be used for communication but had no connection anywhere, he laughed, "I know you want me to say its my penis that wants a connection." Momentarily stumped by this reply, I noticed that his stomach, as well as mine, was growling. Contrary to my usual way of responding, I also laughed and said, "We are both guessing wrong about each other, but our stomachs understand something. They are rumbling at the same time." Val Brewster was thrilled. Accustomed to paying attention to the minutest detail of his musculature, clothing, and digestive system, he had noticed the same phenomenon, our companionably noisy stomachs. "What could this mean?" he, rather than I, asked this time.

Still want to sleep every time he shows up. It starts the minute I set eyes on him. What is he, what am I, escaping from? He doesn't appear to be sleepy at all. On the contrary, lately he has been bright eyed and bushy tailed. Bushy tailed? Yes, the car telephone! He wants to make contact by land and by air, he says (by mouth

and by penis?). What am I thinking here? Is the transference becoming erotized? If so, are we making progress? Or has this to do
with being allowed to have a penis here, or to help him grow one?
His first sexual encounter with the nameless hooker was by mouth.
Is talking a dirty, forbidden activity for him? And who am I?

There is something vaguely disquieting coming up, though I
was pleased with his enjoyment of his borborygmi, somewhat less
with my own spontaneity. What in the world possessed me not to
think first . . . . though there was something playful in the air, as
though we were sharing something nice. . . . Freud's early papers
come to mind, the early ones candidates always find too simple
. . . . maybe because they're too simple . . . . maybe there was
something on the border of psyche and soma here, some ancient
place where mentation begins. What did Freud (1895) say? The
experience of satisfaction "[is brought about] by *extraneous help*
when the attention of an experienced person is drawn to the child's
state by discharge along the path of internal change. In this way
this path of discharge acquires a secondary function of the high-
est importance, that *of communication. . . .*" (p. 318).

But what does he communicate to me? That I am able, and
perhaps too willing, to go back to that early time where I also
experienced satisfaction? Even so, his mother seems to be somewhat in the background right now. Seems when she isn't cleaning,
she's busy monitoring his phone calls. Maybe it is easier for him
to recall the sensation of satisfaction, rather than the person who
was responsible for the satisfaction. My own conflicts with mother
reactivated?

Recovering the Memory of Incest

During the session after our mutual stomach-gurgling, Mr.
Brewster created an entirely different atmosphere. Rather than
shuffling in with bent head and plumping himself down on the
couch, he marched in with a gleam in his eye and smiled at
me before sitting down. "I felt good last time, more like I had
ate a good meal here or something." Taken aback for the
moment by his ungrammatical speech, I merely looked at him.
"I know," he continued, "I'm not supposed to say these things
to you or ask you how you feel. But it was like, you know, like
we ate something togedder." Then he took to the couch,
enlarging on his fantasy that we had eaten a meal together. He
told me about all the foods he liked, special meals his mother

cooked for each family member's birthday, and the many gour-
met dinners he had to attend with his father's customers on
his father's boat. Toward the end of the session, he told me
that once again his mother had exhorted him to "make up his
mind. If he wanted to be homosexual, that was okay with her,
only he should leave her alone already and get on with his sex
life. And anyway, his analysis cost too much." In what seemed
to be a reflective mood for him, he added, "She shouldn't say
that to me. Don't she want me to be a man?" On leaving, he
asked me if I had noticed anything different about him. While
I still wondered if he meant his unusual use of language, he
pointed to a new and obviously very expensive pair of sneak-
ers. I had a sudden image of him as a small boy begging for
approval, and I decided to admire his footgear. Again the
borborygmi occurred.

Wondering what sort of an analysis this would turn out to
be, I actually anticipated Mr. Brewster's next session with lively
curiosity. Apparently he had similar feelings. He reported the
following dream: His car (his graduation present) was in an
indoor garage, next to a sailing boat. He fills the car up with
gas until it overflows. It leaks all over, and he bites off the
nozzle, which makes it stop. A guy in the boat next to him also
has this kind of trouble, although his boat doesn't need gas
but wind. He linked this dream to the borborygmi and
explained to me that the gas represented flatulence, which he
often experienced because he ate too much in order to please
his mother. His ebullient mood vanished. He began to wonder
if he and I were "farting together." Twisting and turning on
the couch, he was clearly uncomfortable but unable to associate or to discuss his comments. He left crestfallen.

The following sessions were cluttered with a barrage of
dreams. These dreams all had oral themes. In the dreams, he
drank out of catsup bottles, spewed filth out of his mouth, committed fellatio with a boy, then with a woman, and saw himself
gorging at family feasts. He was deeply offended when I suggested that we work on one dream at a time and save the others for later. We worked out a compromise. We would work on
one dream of his choosing, and he would write down the others
for later work. While we were working out this compromise,
the mutual chorus of borborygmi could not be ignored. I
conceptualized them as signs that we were mutually engaged

in important psychic work just at the border between physiologic and psychologic experience. I said, "I think that perhaps you are remembering something of your babyhood." He was perplexed about this partial interpretation and denied vehemently that the borborygami could have anything to do with early times "because he was making progress." With all the work on the dreams he had forgotten to tell me that he had "went out with a girl." By now, I knew that Val Brewster fell back on ungrammatical speech patterns when his feelings were aroused. But I was at a loss to explain why a regression during the session should appear in just this form, which was inconsistent with Mr. Brewster's background and did not seem to point to the emergence of a body memory (Siegel, 1988; Siegel et al., 1996). My own associations conjured up a longshoreman or a sailor. Another characteristic of Mr. Brewster's interaction with me was that he found it difficult to use metaphors or analogies. He himself felt that he "missed a beat" every now and then and did not understand what I or others said to him. Despite this fact, he treasured his dreams, though at times he derided himself for believing in "such junk." During such times, he would angrily accuse me of wasting his time. Our experiencing borborygmi together seems, however, to have been a cornerstone for building a strong working alliance. No matter how painful the material eventually became for him, Val Brewster kept pushing himself forward, declaring he wanted to be a man and do the things men do.

In the meantime, his sister Janette also finished college and came home to live. A psychology major, she decided that her brother needed adverse conditioning to rid him of his homosexuality. When he angrily declared that he was not homosexual at all, she arranged for him to meet some of her friends. One of them, Pam, liked Val. He dated her several times but found their outings both boring and frightening. He reported his unease in finding a topic of conversation and almost panicked when she expected to be kissed at the beginning and the end of each date.

Pam took a job as lifeguard during the summer, and Val decided to give tennis lessons at the same exclusive club. This led to teasing by the family, who were convinced he would have simply whiled away the summer if it hadn't been for Pam. He, however, felt the renewed need for male companionship. He realized that he "didn't know the first thing about being with a girl" and hoped to learn this from the young men he met at the club. He bought them drinks and in every way tried to emulate them. His friendly advances were rarely reciprocated. He thought this rejection might have to do with the fact that he secretly measured the size of his penis against those of the men he met while they were in the communal shower. The more he became aware of his father as being emotionally absent from the family, the more he longed to be with men.

As the family stepped up their teasing about his supposed love affair, he was so overcome by resentment and guilt at not satisfying the requirements of his family that he arranged for a group trip to the city where he had found the nameless hooker. But these counterphobic measures helped little to alleviate his mounting anxiety. At the last minute he reneged and let his companions go to the city without him. When he told me about this he was terribly upset. Pam wanted to "tongue kiss." He now felt that he had missed out on "practicing" with someone so that Pam would never know how inexperienced he was. He reported the young woman to be totally devoted to him and relished her admiration of him. In the meantime, he began to feel more and more assaulted by the physical presence of his sister in the house. He felt he now had two mothers who bossed him around. The expected appointment to a good job fell through. He used this as an excuse to distance himself from Pam, claiming that he could no longer afford to wine and dine her.

But Pam was not to be deterred. She came to see him at home and broke into his routine of eating large dinners with the family, jogging, and then watching TV until bedtime. He felt she had robbed him of something. He was not sure of what. A dream provided part of the answer. In it, he was in my office, where I advised him to masturbate because that way we would find out how he got to be the way he was. The question of masturbation bothered him greatly. His mother had berated him when she first found signs of nocturnal emissions on his sheets. Since then, he had worn jockey shorts to bed. He kept returning to the intrusion into his evening ritual represented by Pam. It became clear that sitting in front of the TV set with his pants tightly stretched across his genitals represented a form of masturbation. He brought with him a sex manual and tried to discuss "techniques" with me, all the while apologizing for talking "dirty" in front of me. Another dream portrayed his sister as sitting in his room and masturbating. She had a penis. He was very interested to see it. But he first had to slay a dragon with a sword. Eventually, he threw both the dragon and the sword overboard.

Interpretation of this dream unlocked a number of childhood memories. During less affluent times, the family had taken vacations together and the children had to sleep in the same bed. During such times, they played "doctor" and evolved a complicated game in which they undressed each other. This game persisted until one day Mr. Brewster noticed the string of a tampon hanging out of his sister's vagina. He reported that he had felt nausea then and that he became nauseated now when he saw or smelled evidence of his mother's or sister's menses. He hoped that someone else had "broken in Pam" because the thought of having to deflower her was utterly repugnant. As a matter of fact, the situation between him and Pam was seriously deteriorating, as far as he was concerned. He once again had fantasies about having sex with men in what he now described as "the anal missionary position." He daydreamed about a neighbor's son who seemed particularly attractive to him. Yearning for sexual gratification, he wished fervently to have a homosexual encounter. He attempted to make contact with a school chum who was known to be homosexual. This man took him along to several meeting places. Nothing happened. Mr. Brewster reported himself as unable "to spoil his record." He claimed that meant his abstinence.

In the meantime, he had many fights with his father, which mother monitored and smoothed over. They usually ended with mother holding her son's head against her breast and stroking his hair while beseeching her husband to "go easy on the kid." Father would storm out in a rage to race his speed boat. At other times, he would "say malicious things." What kind of malicious things? Brewster Sr. would accuse mother of spoiling her son, of tying him to her apron strings, and, mysteriously, he would shout "just remember what happened." Indulgent mother declined to give information; as a matter of fact, she was adamant in telling her son to "lay off. Let sleeping dogs lie." Mr. Brewster asked himself repeatedly why "she hadn't protected me like that before. Now it's too late and just makes me feel dumb." Nevertheless, he deeply resented any inquiry into his feelings about the seductive behavior of his mother. He also felt conflicted because mother had advised him to forget the past while he experienced me as actively encouraging him to reconstruct his past. He once again characterized mother as someone who "cleaned before the cleaning lady came so nobody could say the house was dirty."

He also thought his mother didn't like sex and was very innocent. As proof of his mother's innocence, he cited the many times she had not noticed when he and his sister were playing their undressing game under the blankets of their bed. Especially when the family acquired a boat, there was much enforced intimacy. Both adolescents watched as the mother and father got ready for bed. Val Brewster could not remember whether he had seen any sexual encounter between his parents. He doubted that he had because "they probably had sex two times in their lives. Once when they had me and once when they had my sister. And I take after them." He found his father "brutish. He talks dirty, slang, like he wants to turn on Ma, but she don't let him close. Then he begs and whines but she don' relent. The old f. . . ." This time, he noticed how he sounded. Apparently delighted with himself, he stalked out. But another storm was gathering. Because the expected appointment had not come through, Val entered his father's business. When I asked why he had not persisted in finding a job in his profession, he became furious. He began to come late for his sessions and requested many time changes. When I once again refused to change his session to another time—he gave as excuse an appointment with a dentist—he stormed out of the office, vowing never to return. That same evening he called for an extra hour. While I spoke to him about waiting for the next session, I once again noted borborygmi in myself.

> Sometimes Val Brewster's unspoken needs come across so strongly that I feel I'm in the presence of a motherless child. Other times I am thoroughly repulsed. There has to have been more besides the dysfunctional family dynamic. . . . Sometimes he acts as though this is the first inkling he has had of the Oedipus. Mother can do no wrong, father does everything wrong. I often feel I need a shower when he leaves. Why? Instead of trying to bring up Val Brewster, I better find out what those stomach sounds mean. Sometimes his anger is so palpable that I feel fury rising in me as well. Why? Also noted uneven breathing pattern, dizziness, and general queasiness in myself. Could it be incest again?

Surfacing Memories

Val Brewster became enormously polite after he realized how much he had taken in of his father's behavior. Mr. Brewster Sr. was now seen as the exclusive villain. Early memories emerged. Val remembered himself, at about two years of age, standing on the stair landing in his house and howling for his mother. He did this often and was inconsolable when his mother was not present. She was the only one who could put him to bed. He remembered howling when sent to kindergarten, of drawing a picture of his teacher while she was drawing one of him, of being sent to the principal in fourth grade because he had thrown a kid against the wall. Once again, he was confronted with a paternal identification he could not tolerate. The animosity between him and his father reached even stronger proportions. He threatened to move out while the father threatened to cut him off without a penny. Again, mother settled everything by cooking one of her famous meals and made everyone eat themselves into a stupor.

The meals ended with mother caressing Val. After being stroked and being pressed against mother's chest, he found it difficult to be with Pam. She was beginning to press for a permanent commitment. Mother intervened. It was too early for both of them, she said. Then she took her son aside and told him that he "shouldn't lead Pam on." They both knew that he "wasn't ready or able to enter into a marriage." He begged me for direct advice. Did I also think that he was unable to marry? Was it really so important to perform the sexual act? One could always adopt children! He would have liked to stop treatment "because obviously nobody liked to come here," but, then, who would help him out with Pam? Against the wishes of his mother, Pam was still "hanging around and trying to get me." While he was pleased that someone liked him that much, he was also disturbed because mother seemed to become frantic every time Pam appeared on the scene. But Mrs. Brewster did not only experience Pam as a rival. She phoned me and asked me in no uncertain terms to direct her son into "either homosexual or heterosexual behavior. "She didn't care which, just as long as he could figure out whether he was a boy or a girl." My reply that it was my impression her son knew quite well that he was male infuriated her. She did not want his "morals" interfered with; she would tell him when it was time to get married. She knew only too well what men were after, and she tried to preserve her son from the beastliness of other men, including her husband. I saw myself forced to end the conversation by recommending that she take up her concerns with another professional. After that, I declined to take further telephone calls from Mrs. Brewster; I felt that any further interaction with her would jeopardize the already tenuous transference situation of her son.

In the meantime, Val Brewster had found another tactic to divert attention from core conflicts. He professed to be bored and alleviated his boredom by wrapping "chicken skins around my penis and masturbating with that." When I made no reply but waited for further comments, he laughed and said, "Now, if I were to cook them and eat them, that would really be sick, right?" After that, he spent many hours trying to shock me with tales of bizarre behavior that he seemed to manufacture out of whole cloth. He also dreamed that he would like to swallow his own sperm. Understanding him to be narcissistically encapsulated as a defense against the raging oedipal drama and rapidly regressing to the anal stage, I was not surprised when he told me that he put condoms on the handle of the toilet brush in order to masturbate anally. I hoped that none of my personal squeamishness about such revelations came across to him, especially because my borborygmi again were growling loudly. After many such sessions, Mr. Brewster finally burst out, "Are you people actually trained to always be so optimistic and cheerful?" He had noticed the sounds emanating from me and had interpreted them to mean that I was "with him all the way."

A decided shift took place in the sessions after that. Mr. Brewster asked me to call him Val. Instead of trying to shock me, he set to work to uncover what was "holding him back and making him so stubborn and unsexy." Concomitantly, he began to complain of headaches and dizziness; the family physician found that he suffered from hypertension; he contracted many colds, and suddenly claimed to be able to read my thoughts. As a matter of fact, he had begun to understand his own dreams somewhat and was able to reflect on them more fully. He dreamed that he was back in college where two men were watching him and his sister in bed. He jumped up to chase them away, broke clear through the window without hurting himself, and returned to his sister, who said, "Let's take a shower." He awoke with an erection. Surprised and almost frightened by it, he asked me if the dream meant that he and his sister had committed incest. He remembered sleeping in the same bed with her and taking baths and showers together, but he could not recall ever "having done it with her." As he tried to associate to the dream, he reported feeling enormously dizzy, as though he were about to fall off the couch. Finally he sat up and said quite calmly, "No, it wasn't my sister I slept with. It was my mother." He then proceeded to tell me in detail how, before he had reached puberty, his mother had asked him to have cunilingus with her under the guise of "kissing each other all over and playing secret games, just the two of them together." He thought, given his father's brutish behavior, that her wanting to do this was quite understandable. After all, his mother was "a woman in her prime and of course she couldn't endanger her standing in the community by having an affair when her husband was just beginning to make a decent living."

Depression and sadness about the loss of his childhood took over. He had rare bursts of anger against his mother, a woman he was still deeply attached to. He did not manage to confront her. For a while, he thought of confiding in his sister but decided against it because her felt her to be manipulative, and, besides, he did not want to burden her, he said. It was enough that one of the family was a "pariah." During sessions, he kept insisting that he had never really forgotten the many times he had been in his mother's bed, as though now, in exchange for revealing his secret, he had to deny the hard analytic work of three years. It was clear that I had become the abuser in his transference, but, just as he had protected his mother all these years, he now apparently sought to protect our relationship by denying its transferential constellation. He listened patiently whenever I interpreted what I thought was going on but always refuted what I had to say.

Eventually, he managed to have a man-to-man talk with his father. He was told that his mother had been in the care of a psychiatrist for many years, a fact the couple had worked diligently to hide from everyone. When Val inquired what the problem was, his father blushed while mumbling something about "being too close to the children. We all thought you would turn out to be a sissy." Val felt very supported by this discussion. He managed to move in with the patiently waiting Pam, who became his sole confidante. She soothed him when bouts of obsessive doubting clouded his thinking. When he left two years later, he was still troubled by occasional attacks of obsessive ruminations about his past and with hypertensive headaches. He understood intellectually that there might be a connection between the recall of incest and the onset of hypertension but could not acknowledge it emotionally.

Outwardly he presented the picture of the accomplished heir to a well-run business. He tried hard to believe in the image he projected to the world now. He often failed in this but still felt unable to face further exploration of his troubled self. He tried to excuse himself from further analytic therapy by stating that now he wanted to deal with "real-life problems." Because he was able to respond sexually to Pam, he considered his sexuality to be "enjoyable enough." He rationalized his occasional angry outbursts as part of his inborn stubbornness. Apparently what had impressed him deeply during our five-year experience was the fact that, as he put it, "we connected like a mother and child should; I could make believe you were my mother and tease you as though you were my mother." He denied feeling similarly about Pam. When he left, he accused me of being the "same kind of perfectionist" that he himself was. Otherwise I would see how much he had changed. There was no way I could reach his need for fusion with an idealized other, nor the omnipotent denial of physical symptoms. Val Brewster considered himself to be symptom free when he left.

Discussion

Viewed from a developmental point of view, Val Brewster can readily be seen to be suffering from many developmental lags (Stolorow and Lachmann, 1980). His ability to form a strong working alliance and later to enter into various stable transference constellations, however, led me to believe that he had reached the oedipal phase when the real trauma of incest interrupted consolidation of his gains. In addition, he showed the ability to separate fantasy from reality even in his most regressed states; that is, he understood that many of the feelings we needed to discuss were both real in the present and echoes of an equally real past. I am tempted to postulate that he was able to respond more fully because we got in touch with his uncontaminated pre- or nonverbal past through spontaneous mutual borborygmi. He took pleasure in these happenings and saw them as the one "real" connection between us, as though a pleasant body memory informed him that he was safe when these spontaneous sounds occurred. Actually, his whole alimentary tract was in some ways hypercathected. I came to see this phenomenon as a defensive maneuver against the sexual overstimulation meted out by both his mother and his sister. The oral gratification he derived from overeating in the service of pleasing his mother fell into the same category.

Many people speak of having to digest their thoughts. Freud (1918) speaks of his patient's experience as follows: "[his] bowel began like an hysterically affected organ, to join in the conversation" (p. 76). In 1925 Freud linked the intellectual function of judgment to the primitive language of the oral urges: "To negate something in a judgment is, at bottom, to say: 'This is something which I should prefer to repress.' . . . Expressed in the language of the oldest—the oral—instinctual impulses, the judgement is: 'I should like to eat this,' or 'I should like to spit it out'" (pp. 236–237).

Negation was one of the major defenses Val Brewster used throughout, as the case history amply illustrates. He often questioned the reliability of the analytic dyad, not surprising given the many deceits and empathic failures he had encountered in the past. In addition, he was subject to severe castration anxiety because of overstimulation by his mother and, later, his sister, who, unconsciously, had followed in her mother's footsteps. Rather than acknowledging the seductions and his own responses to them, he almost succeeded in psychologically castrating himself by staying virginal. On the other hand, he was very proud of his "purity" despite bizarre sexual fantasies. For a while he even acted on one of them and reported masturbating with a chicken skin. He elaborated on this with glee, like a young child who delights in shocking his parents by picking his nose and then eating the result. He even linked his activity to the oral stage by stating that cooking and eating the skins after such use would be, in his opinion, "really weird."

Many analysts (Deutsch, 1955; Bion, 1963; Frank, 1969) have discussed the meaning of borborygmi in the analytic setting. Most recently, DaSilva (1990) devoted research and thought to borborygmi as undigested facts during moments of analysis when gut issues are being dealt with: "Borborygmi [are heard] accompanied by fantasies of devouring the object and by the hallucinatory sensation of undergoing anew the vicissitudes of experience of satisfaction and of being fed by the analyst" (pp. 645–646). DaSilva goes on to delineate the types and even the tonalities of borborygmi and what they might signify. In his hypothesizing, he is aided by Bion's model of the mind.[1] He stresses that only a peaceful, purring sound communicates the experience of satisfaction. It was this sound that Val Brewster and I emitted.

Lichtenberg (1983) cites findings that raise the question of "the persistence of memory from the presymbolic stage, as reactions from this period may have pathological consequences" (p. 202). Infant research has in part answered this question affirmatively. There is, for instance, little doubt of the infant's engagement with another through eye contact and its satiation after being fed. Stern (1985) states that in primitive societies infants often are fed at the slightest demand (p. 237). DeVore and Konnor (1974) have shown that such feeding keeps the infant at a low level of activation. In contrast, Stern (1985) conceptualizes that in our society "satiation becomes a phenomenon of intensity and drama equal to that of hunger, but in the opposite direction. It may well be that constant experience with exaggerated peaks and valleys of motivational and affective intensity is an adaptive advantage for the infant who is to enter the faster, more stimulating modern world" (p. 237).

Certainly Val Brewster and his family played out their dramas in an oral fashion. Even when mother was no longer forced by her own inner needs to treat her son as a lover, she remained intrusive by insisting that he, and the entire family, eat too much

---

[1] To put it in a very abbreviated and simple form, Bion's model of the mind proposes that so-called undigested facts of sensory impressions, or beta-elements, are communicated via projective identification and are possibly transformed by the ensuing alpha function of the mother–analyst. If they are not transformed, the beta-elements are evacuated by different pathways, such as the soma. If they are transformed, alpha-elements of the patient will be found leading to dream thoughts or building blocks that can construct the thinking apparatus. Of course, Bion does not imply that the analogy with metabolic function is to be taken as a concrete fact. For him, it is a metaphor for the functioning of the mental apparatus.

in order to please her. It was as though her sensuality had taken an entirely oral path that she had to push into her family in order to control her own and their instinctual needs. In Val's reporting, mother's moods and how to alleviate them were always the most important concern. He did not really free himself from the burden of having been mother's lover even after Pam became his wife. Unable really to forgive mother's transgression, he was unable to forgive himself. He always lived in fear of impending catastrophe to be visited on him first by his father, then by his mother. After the incestuous involvement was discussed with his father, however, a reconciliation of sorts between father and son did take place; that is, father stopped having to pay for mother's transgression in Val's psyche. His omnipotence, though, stayed unmodified. Accepting further analytic intervention felt too dangerous to him. Perhaps acknowledging the burden of investigating a grandiose self (Kohut, 1977) was indeed still too dangerous for him.

In some ways Val reminded me of McDougall's (1989) patients whom she so tellingly saw as acting in a "theater of the body." I believe that Val Brewster's many physiologic problems toward the end of our interaction were not conversions in the classic sense of the word but actions designed to hide from himself how much more conflict and sadness, rage, and lust, had to be worked through. He remained very much an actor in his own life in that he still often doubted the authenticity of his own perceptions and experiences. The childhood trauma of incest, although acknowledged, in my opinion remained as a somatic memory expressed in hypertension. Despite his abrupt departure, he felt "more satisfied than ever before. It's you, Doc, who aren't satisfied," he said. He was absolutely right.

SIMON AVITAL

As the date of his wedding moved closer and closer, Mr. Avital noted that a symptom he had lived with for many years was becoming worse. Very much against his better judgment, he found himself forced to visit certain parking lots in the area where he lived because he knew that others like himself would be there with the single aim of satisfying each other's sexual needs. For Mr. Avital, this need consisted of being picked up by a stranger and having the stranger show him his genitals.

Once he had seen the other's penis, he felt at peace, or so he claimed during our first interview.

He was very tall and looked like one of the picturesquely brooding young men in ads for expensive imported clothing. Impeccably dressed and groomed, he folded himself onto my couch with a groan without looking around or looking at me long enough to establish eye contact. He knew that in an analyst's office one uses the couch and therefore he complied with what he thought of as the "regimen" of analysis. Now in his 30's, he had found "the perfect woman for me, a beautiful girl without much experience who was willing to help me through thick and thin." He had told his fiancée that he was "troubled" but did not specify in what way. Apparently, she had not asked for details. They had met on a cruise and had immediately known that they were meant for each other. Initially skeptical, Mr. Avital felt his affection for the young woman, Lara, grow so strong that he asked her to marry him soon after they returned from their vacations. During the early months of their engagement, his need for the voyeuristic outings diminished, another proof to him that Lara was the right person for him. But now, with the wedding date coming closer, he felt inclined "to go to the lot" almost every day. He had been able to distance himself from his ego dystonic symptom by comparing it to certain hazing practices in a fraternity he had belonged to at school and to initiation rites in English public schools he had read about. Nevertheless, he was acutely aware that his practice of merely staring at a stranger's erect penis without gratifying the other's wishes could land him in severe trouble. As a matter of fact, he reported that he had been beaten up when he refused to "go further." He claimed to be fully potent with women and in particular with Lara, who could stimulate him to perform all sorts of sexual marathons. He spent several sessions bemoaning his inability to come to analytic therapy sooner, fearing that his resistance "to something I had known to be good for me for a long time" would seriously damage his chances of conquering his symptom. He claimed to be utterly and completely satisfied with himself otherwise. He earned "goodly" amounts of money as a lawyer and his bride-to-be was a dentist. Therefore, he felt his present and future financial status to be satisfactory. He couldn't think of any other area where he wished for anything at all. He simply wanted to be free of having to go to the lot, period. In contrast to most other patients, he talked without inhibition about his sexual life with Lara and with other women in the past. Apparently, women had always been a great source of satisfaction for him despite his symptom. To me, his active sex life had more the character of a counterphobic defense against homosexuality but, because it was early in the treatment, I held my tongue.

Mr. Avital appeared to be a rather suggestible person. Soon after he started treatment, he claimed to be utterly free of having to go to the lot and praised me as a wonderful analyst. In the presence of such idealizing transference manifestations (Kohut, 1977), I felt it best not to say too much but to acknowledge his relief at not being the slave of his own needs for the time being. During his symptom-free time, Mr. Avital dreamed copiously, tried to understand what he was dreaming about, but became bogged down in his own system of explaining fantasy material. He saw connections and complementary parallels everywhere but without linking them to his own life experience. He seemed to relish fantasizing about a boundariless universe in which everybody loved everybody, but he kept his fantasyland strictly separated from his every day world.

His first dream is of interest. He dreamed that he saw a great many boys milling around an unfamiliar place. He went to his father's house, where he found some bulbs. He planted them in rich soil. He spun an entertaining tale of good and evil being transmitted from generation to generation around this dream and then told me with a smile that he believed that dreams indicated creativity, of which he believed himself to process a great deal. He was aware that I, as an analyst, might disagree with his position, but he just could not bring himself to believe that there was anything else to dreaming. He was, however, willing to accommodate my thought that the dream might indicate that he wanted something from his father. As a teenager he had become converted to Bahai, possibly as a defense against his family, who kept to the ritual of their religion, but not to its spirit, or so Mr. Avital claimed with contempt. He conceded that his particular form of looking at fantasy material might have something to do with Bahai's point of view, namely, that all mankind is one and the whole globe is merging into a world order. He readily agreed that this was a utopian view but told me that he felt better "when connected to all."

He characterized his father as vile and bad tempered; his mother as greedy, manipulative, and possessive. In his own married life, he hoped to avoid the constant fighting and bickering his parents indulged in. He thought that perhaps they had brought this type of behavior with them from their "lower-class upbringing. They didn't have the advantages they gave me," he stated. He professed to be grateful for his private school education and was pleased with his own snobbery. Nevertheless, he considered himself to be a kind and generous person who tried not to hurt anyone "except accidentally, when I couldn't help myself." The question of how to be kind haunted him. He obsessed about whether he had smiled enough at the elevator man in his office building, or whether he had opened the door for an old lady wide enough, and so on. He could work himself into a state of agitation at such times of obsessive doubting. During those times, he felt that anything I said was an intrusion. He experienced these ruminations on and off the couch as "having to reach their own peak without interference from the outside." He confessed that he had been subject to obsessive thinking for as long as he could remember but had not considered it to be a problem because at times this type of thinking would put him "on to something new about a case. I would suddenly remember how to solve a case."

He was very reluctant to discuss his childhood. He had a brother 10 years older than he whom he and the rest of the family professed to despise. Apparently there were many aunts and uncles who liked to take sides in the parental fights. Mr. Avital told many amusing anecdotes about the interference of the clan in the "warfare" between his parents. When I linked his reaction to interpretations as interference with the clan's behavior, he magnanimously agreed "to consider that thought."

The date for the wedding was put off, ostensibly because no suitable apartment had been found, but actually because Mr. Avital now felt that, although Lara was still the woman of his dreams, he could no longer be sure that he was worthy of her. He felt within himself "a place so dark and hidden, who knows what is there?" Over the objections of both sets of parents, the young couple moved in with each other. His parents felt that Mr. Avital was "getting his cake and eating it, too." He was comfortable with the turmoil the move aroused and reported telling his mother "stale cake doesn't taste good." She had been particularly vociferous in her dislike for the joint living quarters.

It was during this time that Mr. Avital began to go to the lot more often than ever. Sometimes he found himself there twice a day. He feared becoming a laughing stock among the people who frequented the place and began to inquire about other locations where he could pursue his voyeuristic needs. When this proved to be difficult because of the distances involved, he thought of paying men to exhibit themselves to him. But that idea was repugnant to him. He now realized that part of the excitement had been to be told how goodlooking and sexy he was and how much the men who spoke to him desired to be his lovers. In desperation, he asked Lara to admire him in the nude. She complied gladly but, to his horror, he found that he could not perform after she had, at his direction, praised the size and the shape of his genitals. He wildly blamed the analysis for castrating him but immediately took the accusation back by saying he really did not mean that at all. What did he mean? That he thought he liked his analyst better than Lara. Of course, he had to undo this confession immediately by stating that he thought himself to be out of line. This time, I decided to be somewhat reassuring and told him that in an analytic setting one could, and even should, say anything one wished to.

I suppose I should feel flattered, but I don't. During this newest sexualization I find him mildly distasteful. There must have been volumes of inappropriate stimulation in his childhood. But not a word of that. He stays in the here-and-now and seems to relish it when I offer transference interpretations. I wonder if he even hears them correctly. Could his hearing be involved? What kind of body memories is he playing out when he goes to the lot? Somehow his mother has something to do with this. Every time he speaks of the men admiring him or when he admires somebody's penis, I get the picture of his mother. He says she is very pretty still. There seems to be a maze of conflicting elements in his identifications. On one hand, he wants to be pretty like mother; on the other hand, he wants to have balls like father. If I had a third hand I'd say . . . . of course, he thinks I have a penis as he thinks mother has a penis and that's what he is looking for. Wonder why I still become offended when somebody decides to provide me with the male genital? He probably is on the way to seeing me as a real object. The sessions are not unduly stormy, so why is my chest pounding like a teenager's? Could I be responding to his sexualization, or do we have incest here again? Why do these people always find me?

Recovering the Memory of Incest

By the time I had been seeing Mr. Avital for two years I was fairly well acquainted with the repeating drama of his family life. The parents required their son and his girlfriend to appear regularly for dinner and outings to the theater and concerts. Just as regularly, mother prodded son to "finally marry the poor thing you've been using all these years"; while father beamed jovially and said that he thought "young folks are not as foolish as we were." The frequency of going to the lot seemed to wax and wane with the tenor of these family visits. It became clear to me that Mr. Avital experienced his mother as castrating and had to supply himself with reassurance by his symptom. But I was not able to explore this thought with the patient. Somehow, he managed to find the time to practice his perversion without arousing anybody's suspicion. Sex between him and the ever-compliant Lara had become perfunctory, and he began to wonder if Lara was indeed the right woman for him. At the same time, leaving her would mean that mother had been right—and that was to be avoided at all cost.

He became depressed and disillusioned with treatment. The initial enthusiasm had worn off, and he now wanted results, wanted to be rid of his symptoms. He had been on the couch for more than a year when it occurred to him that he had felt similarly disillusioned and depressed when his brother was about to leave for college. He described his brother's leaving as "some sort of rent in the fabric of our everyday life. He managed mother's moods. We were still close then." Strangely, Mr. Avital could not lie still when he talked about this time.

He described himself as having been a pudgy child without friends but who was satisfied with his life anyway. He gardened with a passion, a hobby he retained to this day. Wherever he lived, he planted a "little patch of sunshine and blue" and had enlisted Lara in sharing his love for plants and flowers. He reflected nostalgically that mother was not as much of a nag, and that the parents had not fought as much, during the period of his preadolescence. It seemed as though the brother held the key to the riddle of why things had been better then.

But Mr. Avital became increasingly angry now. The lot became "his home away from home," and he scolded me for not keeping him away from it, for being an inadequate therapist, someone who "probably even condoned homosexuality." He had a dream that bothered him so much that, despite his negative feelings, he asked for an extra session, which I was unable to provide. When he gloomily arrived for his scheduled session, he told me that "it had been a close call whether I would come to the office or go to the lot." Only the dream had driven him to his session.

He dreamed that he was in a large apartment building when a window suddenly crumpled and fell on him. It was really supposed to fall on a man who was running away. He again associatively returned to the time when his brother was still at home and wondered why there was no longer a connection between him and his only sibling and why, indeed, his brother never came home any more and only occasionally sent pictures of his wife and children, whom his parents had never met. He began to ponder why this was so but could not come up with any answer. Lara advised him to ask his parents on their next weekly visit why the brother was never home. Mr. Avital glowingly lauded his wife-to-be because she wanted to undertake a reconciliation in time for their wedding. No date had been set. Mother, instead of answering the questions put to her, asserted that Lara was becoming "restless" and that this inquiry into the family's life was her way of reminding them that a wedding was to take place. Mother also cried and "carried on." Still, nothing new had been uncovered. This mystery stayed unresolved until the fourth year of the analysis, when Mr. Avital once again thought of leaving but couldn't because he felt "unresolved" despite the fact that he and his Lara had been married without his brother's appearing on the scene even though he had been invited.

He continued to find summer breaks and even the weekend separations from treatment painful but was also angry at being so "stuck on an analyst whom I don't even know." He had begun to call me when the urge to go to the lot became overwhelming, and the call often helped him to stay away. We had also begun to notice that his need to go to the lot always arose when he and Lara had been particularly close or when he felt successful. He puzzled mightily over why success should scare him.

He began to talk more with his father and, much to his surprise, found his father overjoyed to be included by his son. The family outings were now "divided according to sex," with the two men deep in conversation, ignoring the women.

Lara began to complain, and mother didn't like it either. As a matter of fact, mother had one or two fainting spells in the bathroom. She was found on the floor, hyperventilating and confused. At this point Mr. Avital became even more anxious. He dreamed that a white owl flew through the window of the bedroom where he and Lara were sleeping. The owl turned into a beautiful woman with whom he had "animalistic" sex. He had no association to this and was totally at a loss about what this could mean. He felt that he had "come a long way" because he could now understand that his parents had tried to push him into a way of life they desired but could not have themselves. He understood himself to be the surrogate for "what they had lost." Father had grown up in an orphanage. The large, interfering clan was really the family who had taken the orphan in when he was a teen-ager. They used him as a helper on their farm and to this day could not understand why a man they had taken in as an orphan was making more money than their own sons. Mother's family was largely unknown but was reputed to be difficult. On occasion, his mother would mail a large check to one or another relative but would always make sure that no one ever visited. This side of the family had not been invited to Simon and Lara's wedding either.

Aware that he felt castrated and inauthentic in the role as his parents' surrogate, Mr. Avital still could not account for what the parents had lost or why he had found it necessary to draw an incorrect picture of his extended family. His conversion to Bahai now seemed like the realization of a fantasy about having a perfect family. He also had fantasies of being an orphan himself and then became panic stricken that some calamity had befallen his mother. He would rush to her place of business to make sure she was all right. He could not explain this behavior but noted that, instead of going to the lot, he now rushed off to see mother. In one of his lighter moods he said, "I guess now she is my penis." Lara began to tease and scold him about his extreme attentiveness to his mother. They settled into a routine that required Mr. Avital to call his mother every night before going to sleep and to have lunch with her several times during the week. Lara felt pushed aside and started to create her own scenes. Mother lost no time in pointing out to her son how ridiculously his wife was behaving.

When he went to her house for lunch one weekend, he found his mother naked on the floor of the bathroom, ostensibly having fainted. He picked her up and put her on the marital bed. She slung her arms around his neck and pulled him down to her. Horrified, he rushed from the house. He thought he must have had a hallucination. He called his father to come home and reported that mother had suffered an "attack." After that, mother was dragged from one medical specialist to another. Her son correctly advised psychiatric treatment but was violently rebuffed. As a matter of fact, his parents joined in an effort to persuade him that his analysis had put dirty thoughts in his head. Even the ever-patient Lara could not believe what he told her. He went over the scene repeatedly during his sessions, saying, "The woman had to be crazy. Or is it me?"

During this trying time, he allowed himself to enter into a strong positive transference. He felt protected and "sane" when in session. Eventually, bits and pieces of childhood memories joined together and enabled him to remember earlier seductions by his mother. From the time his brother left home when Simon was nine years old, until about his 12th year, mother and he had often slept in the same bed, with mother stroking him into erection and then crooning to her handiwork as though she had created something that did not really belong to her son but to her. She asked the boy to "ride" her and jeered at him when his erections did not prove strong enough to penetrate her. When he did become mature enough for penetration, the practice ceased.

Mr. Avital spent another three years trying to work through the many ramifications of incest. He vacillated between seeing himself as monster and thinking of himself as the victim of a psychotic mother. Alternately enraged and depressed, he questioned his own sanity over and over again. Finally, he contacted his brother, who, it turned out, had left home because mother had tried to seduce him as well. The brothers met and discussed each other's fate but were unable to overcome the barrier between them. "It was as though mother's ghost was always between us," Mr. Avital reported. He felt both angry at having been abandoned by his brother earlier and grateful to him for having shielded him for so long from mother's unwanted attentions.

At the end of the analysis, Mr. Avital expressed regret at having "put the analyst through hell" but felt cheerful about his future. He also admitted that not having to come for treatment any more was "like having an albatross removed from his neck." Simultaneously, he was able to see that he had transferred some obsessional preoccupations to the process of psychoanalysis. He wondered why he did not feel more sadness about leaving me and decided it was because he "was really taking a piece of you with me inside."

Discussion

That Mr. Avital had escaped the learning inhibitions and more severe disturbance of reality testing usually associated with incest probably had to do with the fact that he had been allowed to grow up undisturbed while his mother focused on the older brother. His self-organization, however, was severely hampered. He did not know to whom his body—in particular, his genitals—belonged. He resorted to voyeurism in order to heal himself. The severe castration anxiety engendered by his mother's claiming his erections as her work and depreciating the strength of his penis made him unsure of just who and what he was. At times identified with the phallic, intrusive, and possessive mother of his preadolescence, he defended himself by the reassuring sight of other men's genitals. He had to confirm and reconfirm that it was indeed men, not women, who possessed a penis. He could hardly bear to work this fantasy through and fled into a positive transference to a nurturing, all-giving mother.

But he had to doubt this perception, too. It did not seem possible to him that he was the only person who truly knew his mother as an incest-ridden woman. He remonstrated with himself and with me that she must have been a good-enough mother to allow him such a carefree youth. He described the urges to go to the lot as sensory experiences of great urgency. He would feel disgusted by Lara's womanly smells, disliked being touched, and could think of nothing else but the lot. Even beatings he received when unable to fulfill the homosexual demands of some of his partners could not deter him from following his overwhelming need. He bound the repeated incestuous experiences in this symptom. His conversion to Bahai constituted another defense against incest. In this religion, equality and the unity of all things is constantly stressed. Here, Mr. Avital could feel free to live out his yearning for oneness with a bountiful earth, which in return represented the nurturing mother for him.

Although he seemed to grow closer to his father for a time, he never resolved his disappointment and anger toward him. When recalling the incestuous behavior of his mother, he asked himself where his father had been, why his father had permitted such activities, and why, even now, when there was incontrovertible proof of mother's behavior, his father chose to seek the help of physicians rather than psychiatrists for his wife. He concluded that father must be sexually dysfunctional and therefore denied what was going on in his household. Mr. Avital himself thought that his passivity in accepting beatings from his partners must stem from an identification with a damaged father figure. When he saw that there was no way to break through his parents' denial, he reluctantly decided to curtail his contacts with them. He began to wonder how I must have felt when he was caught up in denial and disavowal.

Slowly, he learned to appreciate his real attributes and his good fortune in having found Lara. In his profession and in his dealings with people, however, he remained fastidious and overly cautious, possibly in an attempt to assuage a superego that had to deal with the real trauma of incest. But he was able to have deep, sustained relationships, which, at times, were distorted by his masochistic submissiveness. I hypothesized that his mother must have been emotionally available in infancy so that the question of basic trust and the ability to establish stable transferences were never in question. I could not help but reflect that not all of Mr. Avital's difficulties were caused by the incest. Surely the unrealistic, stormy, and counterphobically optimistic atmosphere in the household and the distant, distrustful, and unrealistic attitude of his father must have contributed to his many symptoms as well.

Partially to test his own perception of reality, partially as a last gesture toward acting out within the transference, Mr. Avital contacted his older brother. He was ready to idealize his brother and forge a bond with him. When this proved to be impossible, he recognized his difficulties in separating from ideas and from people. As treatment progressed, he found it less and less necessary to deny and disavow what he felt and perceived. Separation is inevitably connected to individuation. Mr. Avital found it most difficult to give up the protection of the analysis despite railing against it on occasion. He assured me, and himself, that he would return for further treatment should any of his symptoms resurface.

SUMMARY

I have presented the cases of two young men who were incestuously abused by mothers who may have been psychotic. Certainly both women used their family dynamics to structure their boundariless universes. At first glance, the two sons appeared to have something like a narcissistic personality disorder, yet notwithstanding their great investment in their physical appearance and their grandiose assumptions, they did not quite fit that diagnostic category. There rarely, if ever, were the many so-called empty hours of the narcissistic personality. Countertransferentially, I was always aware of the struggle within these men to be themselves, to make sense of fragments of memory, and to connect those memories with perceptions in the here-and-now. Their transferences proved to be quite amenable to interpretation, although Mr. Brewster did not allow himself a separation period from the analysis and from me. His particular pathology precluded the establishment of true autonomy. Much of his inner struggle for psychological survival was based in the oral period, when he was possibly overindulged by a mother who did not know her own boundaries and did not respect those of others. His oedipal conflict remained only partially resolved at the end of treatment.

Both men used denial, isolation, somatic memory, obsessive doubting, and splitting as defenses. There the structural similarity ends. Although on the couch they sometimes experienced states of reverie, those states were not at all like the disassociation of the female analysands discussed in the preceding chapters. Rather, their reveries seemed to be reflective moods accompanied by physical sensations of feeling temporarily protected and therefore able to contact their unconscious with less anxiety. I saw these states as relatively normal somatic remembrances of an adequate infancy.

Because the incest in both cases had taken place rather late in their lives, there were fewer distortions in their egos than in those among the women.

So far, I have written about the similarities between Mr. Brewster and Mr. Avital. Yet these men could not have been more dissimilar. Mr. Brewster did not manage to separate from his dysfunctional family. He saw me as a real object at times and carried this image with him. Therefore, he did not find it necessary to live through an appropriate end to his treatment. In my opinion, he incorporated a protective mother image in the transference and used this to ward off further anxiety. He gave up the idea of autonomy by working with his father rather than following his chosen profession. He continued to have few friends, preferring a rather isolated existence with his wife. Somatic overresponsiveness remained as well.

Mr. Avital, on the other hand, was able to give up narcissistic preoccupations and overcome his castration fears. He was genuinely sorry for his mother and tried to help her. He managed at the end of his analysis to see me as separate from himself, with a life of my own. A somewhat overly strict superego remained at the end of our interaction. I speculate that Mr. Avital's mother must have been able to give more appropriate nurturance to her younger son while the older one satisfied her needs. Perhaps she was also somewhat healthier then. It was never clear just when she had tried to seduce her older son.

Both men functioned on much higher levels than one would expect given their life histories. I suspect this has to do with the fact that their bodies were not intruded into, as was the case with the women I described. The men's sex play with their mothers included passive submission but also very visible erections they were secretly proud of. Neither one of them reported any of the fantasies of fragmentation or showed any of the signs of early castration anxiety postulated by Roiphe and Galenson (1981).[2] This was all the more surprising in the case of Val

---

[2] Roiphe and Galenson have shown that the preoedipal castration reactions, in contrast to the later phallic-oedipal phase castration reactions, not only reflect a threat to the infant's sense of body intactness, but simultaneously are experienced as a threat of object loss.

Brewster, who presented many oral symptoms. It was much easier for the men to acknowledge the pleasurable aspects of their incestuous experiences. There was none of the fear of disintegration experienced by the female analysands. They also much more readily than the women found physical outlets for their overstimulation. Nobody seemed to think it strange for a boy to run and scream and shout or to roll around on the floor or to pick fights with other children; my female patients, on the other hand, reported that they always were exhorted to act like little ladies. But like the women, the men had to deal with parents who condoned and practiced the behavioral expression of conflict. Thus, they were quite certain that at one time or another each person they came in contact with would either seduce them or be seduced by them. Of course included among those people was their analyst. For Mr. Brewster this certainty meant that he had to deny the fact that I was separate from him, whereas, Mr. Avital was able to live through the pain of individuation. I believe that the fact of Mr. Avital's predominantly neurotic pathology throws grave doubts on the assertion that incest always causes borderline structures. As with all trauma, its effect seems to depend on when it occurs and under what circumstances. Certainly the emotionally distant fathers of both men also contributed to the characterologic distortions and developmental lags of their sons.

Chapter 5
Father–Daughter Incest

In the preceding chapter I hypothesized that women who have experienced incest with their fathers are more seriously damaged by the event than are their male counterparts because their bodies were actually, not only symbolically, penetrated. The men who were incestuously used by their mothers also suffered many wounds but tended to be less visibly affected, perhaps because of the cultural expectations of males: A man shows that he is a man by sup-pressing feelings, particularly pain. As a patient put it, "Women have the privilege of letting it all hang out. We men always have to stuff things back in in order to show that we are men." Of course, these are only reflections about surface rationalizations, but the two women I am about to introduce corroborate this assumption. They seeemed positively enamored of their feelings and their expression, lending a somewhat hystrionic air to the general atmosphere of our work together.

The incestuous fathers seem to me to have been just as impaired as the mothers who used their sons. As a matter of fact, I have caught myself thinking that perhaps the incestuous mothers whose children I met were so readily characterized as "crazy" because they were women who were not forced to confront the realities of work outside of their families. These women either worked with or for their husbands or were housewives: No employer supervised them; no coworkers observed their behavior or moods; their families served as a cocoon. Their unusual behavior and mood swings were not hidden, but merely were ignored or denied by their families. No such protection was forthcoming for the incestuous fathers. They appeared to have been the proverbial pillars of society. Nobody, least of all the daughters they abused, could believe that such devoted family men could act in such a destructive manner or could be so impulse ridden and devoid of a sense of responsibility.

The two women whose cases are discussed in this chapter conform more nearly to the usual presenting picture of the incest victim. Early castration anxiety was present from the first day, and body boundary disturbances, motoric enactments of conflict, and fear of object loss were very much in the forefront.

SUE-ANN PIMLICO

Sue-Anne Pimlico was referred by the leader of a self-awareness group for women. In that woman's workshop, Sue-Anne had suffered what seems to have been a temporary break with reality. She could not remember anything at all about this event. She reported that "one minute they were feeling the contours of each other's faces, the next minute she was on the floor howling and screaming." She was told that she had experienced a "catharsis" and was advised to seek help. Deeply ashamed of her "public exhibition," she was glad to come for treatment, she said, because she had been depressed and worried about her marriage for some time. She had ventured into the self-awareness group as a first step toward "doing something about myself." Although she and her husband had been living in their present home for three years, they still felt like strangers in this big city.

They had met and married in a small college in the Midwest that was run by a religious order. A common interest in journalism and photography had drawn them together. Both were the black sheep of their respective families, neither of whom welcomed their union. Feeling both cast aside and restricted by their upbringing, they decided to move East to make their fortune. Both had reasonably good jobs but felt disappointed. They had hoped that the big city would be exciting and welcoming; instead "we stayed home and smoked pot for entertainment like we did in college. We could have stayed on the farm for that," Sue-Ann said. She herself had the well-scrubbed look of a healthy farm girl, but she despised her appearance. She longed to be glamorous and svelte. In her office, men teased her about her buxom appearance. Recently, she had "told them off" and ever since had been isolated in her workplace as well as at home. She was shocked to realize that fighting for her rights and "respect" had landed her in such an unpopular place. Somehow, she had expected praise and recognition for her valor.

She had found the self-awareness group through a newspaper ad. She had an image of herself as strongly identifying with the women's movement, and the acquisition of a "female awareness" matched her expectations. Raised in an "old-fashioned, patriarchal household, she had been taught that being female is a priori shameful." She found the women in her self-awareness group to her liking but was afraid of their open "shamelessness." She had always been taught to keep her feelings to herself, not to "parade them around." The fourth of six children, she felt that she had "gotten lost in the pack" except when she got into trouble. She seemed to have gotten into trouble often and was regularly rescued by her father, who was a deacon in the church they belonged to. Her mother was a "recovered alcoholic," more interested in her AA meetings than in her children, Sue-Ann maintained. She had a close relationship with only one sister. The boys in her family "were all hoods. As long as they had their beer and their girls, they stayed out of trouble and even went to school."

Sue-Ann was glad to have someone to talk to. She readily agreed to a schedule of three times per week and was relieved when I suggested that we begin our work with her sitting up. I was then not at all sure that Sue-Ann would be able to withstand the rigors of psychoanalytic investigation and told her that we would reassess our work together after the first three months. She did not seem to understand what I was talking about. According to her, nothing could possibly go wrong in her interaction with me because she had felt "immediately close and protected, like by a really terrific mother." That she had cast me in that role became clear when she was horrified to hear herself referred to as Mrs. Pimlico. She insisted that she did not know "who that person was, except if I meant her mother-in-law." The question of what she should call me took up a whole session. She finally decided that she would call me differently depending on "how she felt that day" and likened her examination of whether she should call me by my first name, by my full title, or by a yet to be discovered nickname to a game she used to play with her sister while listening to "gloomy sermons in church." Her sister Beth would surreptitiously point to a person or an object in church and Sue-Ann would have to come up with a new name for it that she then relayed in a whisper or with hand signals.

Sue-Ann was only too ready to talk about her life. Easily shifting from past to present and back again, she associated and accepted my first interpretation of her immediate transference reaction. However, she corrected me: no, she did not think that I seemed endowed with a good breast like a good enough mother. She felt that I was almost like a good mother to her in that I listened to her and "let her be." She was particularly pleased that I listened to her many complaints about her husband, Matt. She reported that he was unable to tolerate her feeling states and only sometimes was ready to comply with her sexual demands. By now, her own interest in him was not as keen as it had been. As a matter of fact, she was quite smitten with a young man in her office. He was a quiet type, she said, who still hung on to the hippie style hair and clothing she herself favored. He apparently was as out of place as she herself felt.

The reassessment of our work together at the three-month mark took a surprising turn. Rather than discussing what she had experienced or what she expected from treatment, Sue-Ann, with a smile, reclined on the couch and declared herself ready to be analyzed. She had informed herself about the psychoanalytic expectations for treatment and had prepared this "surprise" for me. Despite thinking of her as Sue-Ann, I did not call her by her first name but tried to avoid addressing her directly, thinking it best to take a middle road between gratification and abstinence. Sue-Ann struck me as needy, prone to regression, and impulsive. While her depressions readily lifted as long as she felt "in touch," she seemed to have taken me for a real object much too rapidly. I was therefore hesitant to have her use the couch. At the same time, she seemed able to have long, sustained, and deep relationships and to be able to seek out and obtain emotional and financial support from her disapproving parents, however scant this supply might turn out to be. The parents had agreed to help with the cost of the analysis, "provided the treatment kept the marriage intact."

I told Sue-Ann that it would be impossible for me to accept such a condition. She cheerfully assured me not to worry. Her parents probably would forget to send her the promised monthly checks anyway because they were engaged in building a new and very expensive house in their town. This house "would be theirs to enjoy without kids messing up everything," Sue-Ann reported. It turned out that she was right.

"I always get sucked in and taken advantage of," she complained and cited many examples both at home, at school, and in her office where this was so. "Why am I such a dunderhead?" she asked herself for the hundredth time. She looked for an answer in the many episodes of having to play second fiddle to her brothers. She also reported harrowing scenes with her mother in which she was accused of being a whore and a dope addict. She was then 12 years old and "had no idea what a whore or dope was. I sure found out quick, though," she said. Identifying with the accusations hurled at her, she began to solicit boys "who were too damn dumb or too young to know what I wanted." (It struck her that her husband acted like that now—he also seemed too dumb to know what she wanted.) Her mother found traces of marijuana in her purse and told her father, who had his own issues with Sue-Ann. His sons had told him what Sue-Ann was up to, had gotten into a few fist fights with boys who spoke badly about their sister, and had finally confided in their father. Sue-Ann got the "tanning of her life on the backside," was grounded for the rest of the year, and was forbidden to watch TV. The parish clergyman appeared weekly and prayed with the mother for Sue-Ann's "spiritual rebirth."

In the meantime, Sue-Ann had found a way to make life bearable. One of her friends nightly brought a ladder to her second-story window so that she could escape for awhile. She was careful not to be seen and regularly took refuge either in the nearby woods or in the homes of girlfriends. She was never discovered. By the time she left for college, she was "thoroughly cynical and disillusioned. Everything my parents taught me turned out to be shit." This statement seemed to me a total contradiction of how Sue-Ann behaved and how she must have appeared to others. Rather than the disillusioned, world-weary vamp she described, she looked and acted like a rather naive girl from the farm. During her descriptions of scenes with her parents I watched for signs that she might be reliving rather than remembering, but I found that she had sufficient distance from these unfortunate, not to say tragic, misunderstandings to work some of them through. She became depressed but managed to mourn the "could-have-been" relationship with her mother.

During this time she had a dream that she found impenetrable by association. She dreamed that she was drug tripping on three microchips. Somebody had put them in her drink. She did not want to drink at all, but she was being chased and followed and therefore had to drink. Fortunately, she met and visited a male friend. She felt strongly attracted to him and he propositioned her. But she said, "I am married to Matt." She sat on a bed and he held her legs and put his face in her lap.

> Curious, I haven't written about Sue-Ann. She seems very familiar to me. I respond as though she were really my daughter, and I feel most protective. Sometimes, when she talks of her parents, her hatred seems palpable and I get the familiar lack of breath and heart pounding. There really has to have been incest behind that halo of pureness her father wears. And that impossible mother, always praying and talking on the phone, calling her kid names . . . . it all falls into the pattern. Careful not to suggest anything. But what else could that dream mean she brought in today. I could hardly listen to it to the end. The old bastard probably fellated her and she liked it.

Recovering the Memory of Incest

The dream of being drugged and warding off seduction by a man to whom she was not married stayed with Sue-Ann like an undigested piece of food. She repeatedly came back to it during sessions but could not make head or tail of it. At that time, her mother, for reasons known only to herself, decided to send her daughter a rather impressive gift of money. Sue-Ann was puzzled to note that she felt disgust and anger instead of gratitude when the gift arrived. She described herself as greedy, of not wanting to share any of the money with Matt, of wanting much, much more. Her regression deepened. She appeared unable to hear what I said but claimed that my office was the only place in which she felt safe. I suggested that she sit up for a while. She thought that was a horrible idea. The prone position on the couch suited her, she claimed. She "could hide there and not be seen." She tried to make herself small and curled up on her side. This became her favorite position, from which she mumbled her grievances. I asked why she had to turn away from me. Her reply was that she was not turning away from me, she was just worried that I would turn out to be like all the rest. Who were all the rest? Matt, her boss, the interesting hippie at work, the clergyman who prayed over her when she was a teenager, and her father. One good thing was happening to her, she told me. She did not have to smoke any pot to feel very, very hazy and good. She could make herself just "swim in warm air and moist clouds and feel very, very sexy" just by assuming her favorite position. She did that at home, too. She was thinking of quitting her job because she needed more time to "think." She was not depressed any more, she claimed. She just wanted to feel "like this always." Her regression and disassociation deepened so much I was tempted to suggest a consultation.

> That teaches me. Don't be smug, smartie . . . . so maybe there was incest, but in the transference *I* am the seducer. She sexualizes so heavily, she seems delusional. What must her life look like? And where is Matt? Why doesn't somebody protect this woman? Good thing she still remembers how she felt here previously. Maybe this will help her through. There is such a strong masturbatory pleasure in her twilight states . . . . what was the experience for her? Incest could not have been so wonderful that she wants to hold on to it . . . . or is she identifying with mother? She surely sees me as the seducer, but a good seducer? How is one a good seducer?

Memories Surfacing

Suddenly, Sue-Ann snapped out of her semidelusional state. Her husband's job was threatened, so that it became doubly necessary for her to hold on to her work rather than giving notice. She felt unduly burdened by this turn of events. She hadn't married him to support him, she angrily wailed. Besides, he was now a total washout in bed. Maybe that was her fault because she often did not wash and made herself presentable only when she went to work or came for her sessions. On the way to one of her sessions, she saw an old bag lady. This made her terribly sad. Perhaps she would become a bag lady in her old age! She sat up on the couch. No, the bag lady was her mother. Mother always took sides against her.

She remembered that, when she was being punished by confinement to the house, she began to spy on her mother "for something to do." Mother would pray a lot, smoke a lot, and then pull down her undies to examine herself. Sue-Ann blushed at the memory. She sighed deeply and went on to tell me how her mother must have thought that she was injured because she would look at her crotch and cry "as though she was hurt or had lost something." Concomitantly, Sue-Ann herself became totally frigid and refused to sleep in the same room with her husband, as her mother had done with her father. Mother and Sue-Ann had discussed these events, both in the past and in the present. I pointed out the identification with her unhappy mother, who apparently also could not arouse her husband. Sue-Ann wished herself dead and came to sessions reeking of marijuana. I told her that this would hinder our work together. Somehow, the working alliance held, and she returned sober, with a dream. She saw herself with a pierced nose with a ring through the middle. In one nostril she wore a stud earring. She wanted a photograph of herself looking like that but, when she got it, she threw it out because it was stupid looking.

When she associated to the photo the "picture I get of myself in the sessions," she was able to accept the defensive aspect of the dream but began to dissociate. She laughingly asked me if I ever joined anyone on the couch and again assumed the curious shrimplike position I described earlier. It was clear that she expected me to penetrate her in some way. This enactment now began to happen frequently. Each time, she emerged out of this state with another piece of information about her past. In particular, she was hurt and angry about how little her mother valued her. "Just because I have no penis, she thinks I'm ugly," Sue-Ann stated on one occasion. Then a whole litany of grievances appeared. She didn't know the right people to help her move forward; she didn't have any influence anywhere; nobody listened to her; every aspect of her life, including sex, was rotten. When I interpreted her penis envy as lack of power, there was a brief respite from her agitated depression that was followed by another bout of dissociation and depression. We had begun to talk about the strange position she chose on the couch when she cried out, "That's how he can get in better." She heard what she had said and set about trying to understand what her words meant. It did not take a great deal of reconstruction to understand that her father had sodomized her repeatedly and that he had "kissed my front to make the hurt in back go away."

After this memory surfaced, Sue-Ann focused on her lack of self-respect. She vacillated between seeing herself as the chosen one among her siblings and as the monster who was probably responsible for her parents' lack of control over their instinctual drives. At times, her self-recrimination became so violent that she could not go to work, fearing that "people can see on my forehead what I've done." This semidelusional statement was traced to a practice of her mother, who, when she suspected a child of telling lies, put her hand on the culprit's forehead and said she "could feel the lies percolating." I finally told her that even Hester Prynn had been forgiven in the end. She could accept this brief interpretation and realized that she was punishing herself for enjoying the perverse pleasures her father had offered. It took much longer for her to accept that her parents had been remiss in their parental duties, that what her father had done to her was a crime, and that her mother was an accessory to the fact. But as she began to see how identifications with her self-serving parents permeated her every breath, she began to distance from the major trauma in her life.

Sue-Ann was finally able to leave therapy after eight years. She struggled valiantly to build a life that was not overshadowed by her past. She was aided by her husband, who became emotionally accessible after entering psychoanalytic therapy under pressure from her. On leaving, she felt that she had not dealt with her separation grief sufficiently but that she wanted to "try to deal with this by myself. I can't be a baby with you all the time although I would like to be."

Discussion

Unconscious grandiose fantasies of having incestuously controlled her father and her mother alternated with episodes of painful lack of self-esteem and shame when Sue-Ann presented herself for treatment. Vulnerable to slights of all sorts, she always teetered on the brink of depression and often sank deeply into states of depersonalization. She was, however, able to enter into an almost immediate transference, which I at first took to be an idealizing one. But she had entered the oedipal phase sufficiently for her to project a need gratifying image onto me, though this quickly showed itself to be a defensively held position. As long as she could admire me and stay connected to her fantasy of a perfect mother, she was able to function. She called this "being in touch." At other times, she temporarily lost touch with reality and entered into a haze of frightening disassociation. Her initial lack of friends seemed to have had the function of protecting her from overstimulation, which then could lead to the feared somatic and motoric memories both on and off the couch. When her expectations were not met, her shame reactions had little or nothing to do with an overly strict superego. Rather, they reflected narcissistic rage (Kohut, 1971).

Whenever her fragile self was in danger of fragmenting (Kohut, 1977), she resorted to secret masturbatory fantasies that appeared to include a blurring of gender identity. During the many hours she spent in her symbolic position of the couch, she alternately fantasized being like her incestuous father or being like her dispairing, masturbating mother. She sometimes expressed the wish that somebody would do to me, her analyst, what had been done to her so that I could understand her even better. During those sessions, she appeared to experience me as unable to protect her as her mother had been unable or as part of her own helpless, pinned-down self. But after these sessions she always expressed relief and acknowledged that I was "really there for me." She recalled the many hours she spent either spying on her mother or trying to cicumvent her parents' punishment. The memory of these behaviors helped her to work through her wish for parents who could be idealized and taken as models. But, unlike patients beset by narcissistic personality disorders, she never lost touch with the working alliance and, hence, the transference. Clinging to what she termed my belief in her, she allowed herself to regress both as a defense against remembering incest and as an invitation for rescue.

As she came to understand the deep impact on her unconsolidated self of her father's perverse sexual demands, she was at first not shocked but ashamed. Shame was one of her preferred modes of ordering her universe. She was ashamed of her looks, her husband, and almost all the things she did. Being ashamed of something made it possible for her to look at it, reflect upon it, and then put it out of her mind as not suitable for herself. The entire first phase of her treatment was taken up with exploring the reasons for her isolation and disappointment. After she was able to integrate the envy that was the opposite of her shameful feelings, she at first regressed but permitted herself to stay in touch with the beneficial image of an analyst who believed in her.

The counterpoints shame–envy again had to be worked through on an object-relational level when Sue-Ann remembered incest. At first, she could not believe her own recollections; then she doubted that her father was capable of such actions; and, lastly, she could not fathom that her mother would permit such behavior. She needed at all costs to hold on to an image of good parents who were simply overly strict. But her own bodily responses, dreams, and recollections finally enabled her to see that it was not she who had transgressed, but her father. As a result, she gave up her omnipotent fantasy that she was the cause of all her family's ills. This event, in turn, helped her to establish firmer body boundaries, an enhanced sense of self, and, above all, more realistic and less exhibitionistic and manipulative object relationships.

CINDY WAUGH

Cindy Waugh thought of herself as a thoroughly modern woman, liberated and "in every way equal to men." She presented herself for treatment because she felt depressed "not about all that fantasy stuff but about the fact that my position is disappearing. I'm facing a midlife crisis and all by myself." She seemed uncomfortable after this opening gambit and at a loss for words. She had come for psychoanalytic treatment because one of her friends had obtained "peace" during a psychoanalysis and was busy recruiting her friends for such intervention. Ms. Waugh remarked that she was accustomed to the best and from what she had read, "psychoanalysis beats all the other forms of treatment." She was surprised that I did not join in a paean of praise for the profession and tried to quiz me about the expectable length and depth of treatment, what my goals would be for her, and if she could expect any further psychological discomfort. I explained as mildly as I could that, in the psychoanalytic form of relating to oneself and others, a different form of thinking prevailed, different from the businesslike, rational way she was used to, and that therefore I could give her no guarantees other than that I would be available to her as an analyst. She appreciated this statement as "forthright" and launched readily into telling me about herself.

Now a handsome, somewhat androgynous-appearing woman in her late 30s, she had come to her present, quite prestigious job on invitation. But now her industry was threatened by computer technology and many foreign imports so that she, as key account executive, feared being out of a job soon. Before this dire event could occur, she wanted to make a career change and was prepared either to go to graduate school or to receive further training. She was surprised to note that nothing really appealed to her outside of her known business world. She felt herself to be "stuck in a job that is going nowhere and in a relationship that is going nowhere." She thought these stalemates had to do with "becoming old. I would never have settled for one creeping, deadly boring man if I weren't afraid." She failed to understand what her fears might be other than that she was getting old. She recounted how, as a young woman, she had arrived at her first job to find herself courted by many men. She thoroughly enjoyed being taken to glamorous places and on clandestine weekends; she felt that being unincumbered left her free to pursue her career. She repeatedly assured me, and perhaps herself, that she wanted no permanent relationship, relished her independence, and did not want any children. If "men can screw around, then women can, too," she asserted. In her present relationship she felt helpless because "my man, Pete" expected her to be faithful, to be emotionally and actually available to him, and to help him entertain his customers.

Cindy resented this role because it reminded her too much of her mother. She sketched a picture of a "typical American family." Father had a more than decent job and thought of himself as a good provider. He didn't spend much time at home, and was happiest when hunting with other men. His hobby was collecting guns. Both his daughters and his wife were angry about the amount of time he spent with his collection. Mother was a dutiful housewife. "The only person with any spunk in the family" was, according to Ms. Waugh, her maternal grandmother, who now lived in a nursing home. Ms. Waugh made it her business to visit her whenever she could. Apparently grandmother had championed her spirited granddaughter and even sent her money when she "defected." As a teenager, Ms. Waugh had won a travel contest. When her free vacation was over, she simply never returned home. At first, she asserted that her parents didn't "give a hoot" when she did not come back. Later, she was able to recall that mother had come to visit her and begged her to return. Even after she had become successful, Ms. Waugh never had a visit from her father.

Ever efficient, Ms. Waugh prepared herself beforehand for each session. She came equipped with material that seemed timed. She'd speak for about 10 or 20 minutes, politely wait for a response from me, and then go on with her very organized reporting. She responded to my silence by saying, "I don't know what that's supposed to do for me, but I know that shrinks don't talk much." This recurring phrase seemed to be a refrain that reassured her. Everything was running as it was supposed to, she thought. She was profoundly puzzled by my occasional inquiry about her transference state. Of course she liked me. Why else would she come here? But even if she did not like me, wasn't it good for her to come and talk so often about herself? I tried to make a distinction for her between talking about herself and talking about her self. But that was something she did not want to countenance. She declared such thoughts to be too deep for her to understand. She knew from her friend that you are supposed to love, or hate, or have some feeling about your analyst, and she did like me, but what was all the fuss about? This disavowal now became the standard answer to my interpretive questions. Ms. Waugh was so intent on preserving her "free woman" persona that she did not allow herself to look at the roots of her behavior.

Curious. The sessions are so flat and monotone I should be bored to tears, but I am not. I would think another NPD. Reminds me of *Nationalsozialistische Partei*. I remember some of the Hitler Youth kids who had to go out and collect money for the party. It was bitter cold, and their thin uniforms did not keep them warm; their knees above their kneesocks turned blue. They had that same frozen demeanor. I used to feel sorry for them until I found out that some of them turned in their parents as traitors. Maybe that's why they had to look so flat, as Ms. Waugh does. How she must hate her parents! So, not a narcissistic personality but someone who has been brutalized. Not so astounding, given her style. Her so called independence is highly provocative. Who is she to me? There is something so familiar about this supposedly uninvolved, liberated woman. She has guts all right, but what does she do with her feelings? And did she really just run off like that? In a way, she reminds me of myself when I came back to the US . . . . but I was then 17, she is now in her late 30s. A teenager in her 30s. . . .

Recovering the Memory of Incest

After many sessions spent in her self-imposed isolation, a dream portrayed vividly how Ms. Waugh really felt. In it she comes home to her apartment. There is no one there. She goes across the hall to see if there is anyone in the building, but there is no one anywhere. She decides to turn a light on but finds that she cannot do so. This dream moved her to tears. Angrily, she corroborated that this was how her life felt to her, lonely and without any light at all. Nobody was willing to help her, ever. That's why she had to come and lie on my couch for a lot of money. I replied that now perhaps we could look at why there was no one in her apartment, because she apparently wanted someone there. This interpretive comment brought her to a screen memory: When she was five years old, the family went on vacation. She ran into a door jamb, and her father spanked her because she had not been careful.

In recounting this anecdote, allowing herself to portray her father in a less distanced way permitted her to give up some of her grandiose demands on herself. It was as though admitting to herself that she did want to be loved and was not self-sufficient, that her family was indeed unempathic, permitted her to shed her shell. Ms. Waugh now began to speak more feelingly about her family and about the man Pete. He had invited her to take a tour of Europe with him where he had to travel on business. But it soon became clear that she would have to pay her own way. Ms. Waugh found it disturbing that it never had occurred to her before to ask who would pay for what during previous encounters with men. She seriously wondered if perhaps I was suggesting a traditional female role for her but recognized that she had been acting more like her father than her mother. She reassessed her previous decision not to have children and now began to mourn "the babies I could have had but was never allowed to live." She recalled having had two abortions. "I didn't know who the father was," she said. That's another reason why I had to get rid of it." She began to question her entire life style up to now and remarked repeatedly that "free love is not free. The price is high." On occasion, she sank back into her omnipotently distancing shell. Then she would accuse me of not being moral because I did not comment negatively about her past behavior.

In the transference, she permitted herself to think that maybe I was similar to her grandmother. She idealized this woman, who was very critical of her only daughter, saying openly that she was disappointed that "a girl with all the advantages settled for a bum like Cindy Waugh's father." The old lady made it very plain that her son-in-law was to keep his distance from her, and she willed her possessions to her two granddaughters. Ms. Waugh reported that she always had a good laugh with grandmother when this lady started to berate Mr. Waugh. When a visit to her hometown and grandmother was eminent, she looked forward to such a gabfest. Just before her departure, both her boss and her man, Pete, confronted her within the same week. The former wanted to warn her that the organization they both worked for was about to be merged with another company and Pete wanted to "realign our relationship." When she asked if that meant he would marry her, he answered that he had thought about it but, given her refusal to have children and her former life style, he doubted it. What he wanted right now was a permanent companion who did not make waves.

Ms. Waugh was disconsolate. She felt that she was a "mega failure." Her perception was that she had tried to live life her own way and had failed. Therefore, in the analysis and outside of it, she had tried to restructure her life "according to the rules." And what had that brought her? Nothing! She now felt that she had been right in not attempting a monogamous relationship before Pete. She felt she did "even worse with him than with the other guys, whom I liked only in the sack." She bewailed her "lack of relationships skills," which, she felt, she could never have learned from her family where everybody always compared her- or himself as inferior to everybody else. That was considered to be good manners." She also told me for the first time that her mother and father slept in separate rooms. This made her very thoughtful. Father was "macho."

Did he perhaps have a mistress? She immediately withdrew that statement as highly unlikely. After all, it was father more than mother who had scoffed at her way of life.

She recalled an episode at the end of one of her visits home. Father had taken her to the airport. It was a long, silent ride. She was angry at father for having gone hunting while she was home, only to return at the last minute to ask her if she would finally settle down and be "decent." When she got out of the car at the airport, father wanted to shake her hand. He tried to put a $100 bill into her hand. But "I felt like a whore and threw the money in his face." She was unusually agitated when she recounted this happening and could not understand why she had not felt "triumphant at having bested him." The thought struck her that perhaps she had been promiscuous in order to best her father. This too seemed an outlandish thought to her. Her father wanted her to be married, she was sure of that; so why would she best him with her sexual behavior? She decided to ask Pete to go home with her this time, feeling she needed an unbiased observation of her family. He was surprised but readily acquiesced. At home, the family immediately saw in him their future son-in-law and treated him as such. Ms. Waugh was disgusted. "I told them he is no husband material, but they made up their minds and that was that. As usual, nobody asked what I wanted or felt. My father invited him to go hunting, but Pete fortunately is not into killing things."

This visit made her reminisce about the years just before she left home. A young football player had asked her for a date. It was a holiday weekend. Her father's cronies were visiting him, and all were in a congenial "beer fog" when the young man arrived. Rather than calling his daughter or escorting her date into the house, the older men sat the young man on a barrel, shone a search light in his face, and gave him the third degree about why he wanted to date Cindy Waugh. She recalled several other episodes in which father managed to "protect" his daughter from being influenced by other males. The more Ms. Waugh began to recall, the more she asked, "Where was my mother?"

She often cried during sessions and said she was unable to make decisions. A series of dreams frightened her further with vivid imagery of surgery being performed in her mouth. At work, she sometimes forgot where she was and was glad that this employment was going to end. Nonetheless, her relationship with Pete seemed to improve. There was talk of moving in together, something she had never permitted before. Berating herself for being weak, she thought perhaps she would allow Pete to come closer to her because she now feared being alone instead of relishing it. As she clung more tightly to Pete, she began to enjoy a rather negative transference state. She began to doubt whether psychoanalysis had helped her and whether I was really equipped to deal with her. She experienced me as having taken her independence and autonomy from her and of having reduced her to a weakling. These recriminations seemed forgotten when she appeared for her next session.

> I can't believe it. Another one. I'm sure this one has also been abused by her father. My heart races; I can't breath and have to consciously make myself calm in sessions. She acts like a border-line but really isn't it. This regression is in the service of lifting the repression . . . . I hope. When she yells at me, she feels like an angry, frightened baby who wants Ma.

Recovering the Memory of Incest

Despite her disavowal of the efficacy of psychoanalytic treatment, Ms. Waugh continued to immerse herself in her own history. She admitted that she really did not like sexual intercourse. The excitement she felt had "other sources, I don't know which." In a dream she was blowing her hair dry when she suddenly noticed that she had both a penis and breasts. Frightened by the graphic images in her dream, she began to question if she was truly female. She tried to laugh this dream off but found herself drawn back to it associatively. She began to blame her mother for what she now saw as her lack of femininity and scheduled trips home, which she could not really afford. Each time she came back with another story of her father's bullying behavior. She began to suspect that he must have "bullied me also. He didn't want other males near me. Why? He didn't own me. But how could he have done *that* without my remembering." I asked her what she meant by *that*. She seemed not to hear me. Instead, she spoke about a fire burning on a mountain and having to save some horses. She saw herself putting a wet cloth over the horses' eyes and then leading them out. This vivid daydream led her to speculate that her father might have used her sexually. She herself interpreted the fire on the mountain as her prepubertal feelings. "The pubic hair is called the mons

veneris, isn't it? That means a mountain, right?" she asked piti-
fully. Overstimulated by her father as a child, she had no way
of finding relief for bodily tensions. She could not bear being
near any man at this point and asked Pete to have patience with
her. On another trip home, her grandmother was not surprised
when she asked her if she thought it possible that her father
had misused her. Grandmother laughed. She had suspected
similar events herself but had not been able to convince her
daughter that she should pay closer attention to what was going on between her husband and her child. She claimed that
the estrangement between herself and Cindy Waugh's mother
had had its origin in that time. As Ms. Waugh put it, "I always
wondered why Grandma lived in that home and not with us, I
mean, with my mother and father. They always said she was too
ornery to live with a family."

Gradually, and with much doubting during stressful sessions,
she recalled the details of her abuse. Starved for affection, she
would follow her father whenever she had the chance, even into
the bathroom. It was there that most of their interactions occurred. He liked her to be absolutely still, warning her that
mother would be furious if she found out, that she must never
learn of their secret together. He liked to wash her hair with
beer and then smear the child's body with the liquid, which he
would then "slurp like a dog until he could put his big, fat, ugly
thing into me. It hurt. I don't know why I held still." She blamed
herself for being a "miniature Lolita" and accused herself of
seducing her father. Her initial doubts disappeared when she
began to realize that "her flight from the family and from men
was really a flight from that beerbellied slob." At times she was
so furious she wanted to go home and confront her father; then
again she was worried what her mother would say. Mother appeared incredibly fragile to her and as unable to understand
what her duties and functions as a wife and mother should be.
When she did marry, Ms. Waugh invited only her grandmother
to the wedding. She continued to visit her mother and grandmother but never entered her parental home again.

Like other patients with similar trauma in their backgrounds,
Ms. Waugh found it difficult to believe her own perceptions.
She gradually began to believe herself when new physical sensations arose during intercourse. Her relationship with Pete did
not last, but she found another, more suitable partner whom
she eventually married. Pete found her new, often volatile feel-

ing states intolerable and did not want to hear about her injuries. He began to be "nauseated" by her. Ms. Waugh, however, was certain that she would not have been able to enter into the relationship with her husband if it had not been for her "practicing period" with Pete. But sex with Pete was "a wild romp with me on top and getting off and out as quickly as I could." In contrast, making love with her husband was "delicious and slow. We both love it and are able to relax afterward instead of jumping up and looking for more and more stuff to do."

Her search for another career ended when an executive with whom she had been dealing for years offered her a highly rewarding position. She was pleased for many reasons but especially because this offer meant to her that "even in those screwed-up times I did some things right, like my work." Sadness for the children she could have had stayed with her until the end of our work together. Feeling her body "had been tampered with and misused enough," she did not wish to enter any fertility programs. Adoption did not appeal to her, although she began to send money to various organizations that care for children in distant lands. I found it interesting that even when she had reached this evolved level, her body signals were the beacons by which she oriented herself as to the reality of her memories.

Discussion

At the beginning of her treatment, Ms. Waugh appeared to understand life in terms of narcissistic gratification or injury. She defended herself against pain and emptiness by not allowing feelings to surface, as though she feared fragmentation. Her object relationships were attenuated, serving only the function of gratifying immediate, sexualized needs. I came to understand Ms. Waugh's seemingly insatiable search for sexual gratification as her way of dealing with the unbearable tensions engendered by early and frequent sexual overstimulation and abuse by her father. She recovered first the bodily sensations accompanying incest, then the affects surrounding the frightening but also exhilarating sense of being father's favorite.

At first, she seemed hardly analyzable, staying in the concrete narrative of current events in her life. But it became clear that she was not afflicted by a narcissistic personality disorder; she showed none of the expectable arrogance or coldness, nor the vulnerability shown by such patients. I was impressed by her range of defensive maneuvers, which indicated at least the presence of inner structure. Along with distancing, warding off, and regressing, she used displacement upward, as in the dream in which she saw her mouth operated on.

Identification with the aggressor was also clearly present in her acting out her trauma over and over again. She rarely became dissociated. I can recall only one instance during which she was so overcome by the overwhelming tension and anxiety of surfacing memories that she became confused about where she was. During that time in the transference, she felt me to be the abuser, especially when the question of her sexual identity arose. She was both frightened and repelled by the thought of herself as a hermaphrodite. It was especially painful for her to realize that mother had failed in her protective functions. The separate bedrooms of her parents had always seemed "natural" to her but now took on a special significance.

During these stressful times in the analysis, her working alliance and her grip on reality never faltered. Although not always able to make decisions then, she weathered a separation from the only man she had ever had a lasting relationship with and, not long after, found a man for whom she had respect as well as love. Her crucial daydream in the office struck me as negatively oedipal in nature. She had to save the father/horse by putting a wet cloth over his eyes. She was the rescuer, not the one saved. In associating to the daydream, she recognized the horse as a father image because, she said, her favorite position during sexual intercourse was on top. "But horses are ridden on top, right?" She elaborated that she did not really ride her father, rather that he had ridden her. She had learned to read and to understand her own unconscious imagery by this time. The flatness of voice and clumsy way of speaking that were evident in her early sessions were completely gone. She now expressed herself with the tact and grace of an accomplished woman.

I am to this day of a divided opinion about Ms. Waugh's handling of her aggressive drives. I found it totally understandable that she did not want to face the man who had wrecked so much of her life. What good would an open confrontation do? She recognized her father as "mentally ill" but had no inclination to forgive him. She felt justified in being angry. She suggested to her mother that she enter counseling "to deal with Pa." But mother found that idea frightening. Used to taking the path of least resistance, she cried with her daughter about the incest, did not even doubt that her daughter was right, yet she chose to stay in the relationship with her husband. What Ms. Waugh did effect was a reconciliation between her mother and her grandmother, who were united in their support for her.

SUMMARY

Both women whose case histories I have presented left no doubt in my mind—and in my countertransference—that they had experienced actual, overt incest with their fathers. They had many features in common. Above all, they both expressed conflict in physical, motoric forms, which, according to Dewald (1989), is a hallmark of the actual, not fantasized, occurrence of incest. Symbolic motor patterns and motor behavior have been interpreted as belonging to early phases of development and therefore as being part and parcel of the narcissistic and borderline pathologies (see Kestenberg, 1967; Kernberg, 1975, 1976; Stolorow and Lachmann, 1980). It is therefore presumed that these patients will be difficult or impossible to analyze. My clinical experience has taught me that people who have a highly active motor drive were not necessarily wounded at an early time of their lives (Siegel, 1984; Siegel et al., 1996). In my opinion, they merely are endowed with a stronger urgency toward physical activity. Concomitantly, a more urgent motor drive does not inevitably connote a lack of desomatization (Schur, 1955).

The distinctive feature of motoric enactment of conflict is that it means something to the patient, even if the patient is at first not aware of the symbolic significance. Thus, the need for motoric discharge alone does not necessarily indicate early psychological trauma, developmental lag, or lack of impulse control (Mittelmann, 1957). Many an analysand plays tennis or golf or takes aerobic classes after each session to deal with the physical discomfort that can be engendered by the prone position on the couch without finding it strange that 45 minutes of being still demands muscular relief. Thus, where and how the motor drive is used by each patient often remains unexplored.

Having hypothesized this much, I would like to extend my argument even further by saying that neither woman I presented in this chapter was classifiable as suffering either from narcissistic personality disorder or a borderline condition resulting from the incest they had experienced. There is no doubt that they had borderline features and had sustained severe narcissistic injuries, but each had formed a stable transference and was able to make use of me, as the analyst, as a constant object despite disappointment and disillusionment. In addition, their affective forms of expression were vastly different. One was highly volatile; the other, overcontrolled, almost obsessive in her need to be "on top." Perhaps their differing styles were due to their native endowment. More likely, it had to do with the kind of mothering they had received. Sue-Ann was at first "smothered" by her mother, then ignored. Her mother liked the state of being pregnant and appeared less interested in her children when they grew older. Ms. Waugh's mother, on the other hand, lived by the clock and handled her baby by the clock. Surely the maternal style of handling their infants left its imprint on these women. Both mothers seemed blithely unaware of what was befalling their daughters. Their lack of awareness leads me to postulate that the ground was already prepared for the incest to take place: it occurred to neither of the women to ask for assistance or protection from her mother when she was being abused. Lack of trust in their mothers' ability to protect them set the stage for the paternal transgressions to take place. Yet the core gender identities (Stoller, 1977) of both women were intact; they even knew what the functions of their femaleness should be and were puzzled by their inability to be like other women. A mitigating factor might have been the adequate preoedipal nurturance they received. In Ms. Waugh's case, this benign environment was enhanced by her grandmother's deep interest in her welfare. Both women were eager to love and be loved. They managed to find partners who helped them to create the emotional environments they craved. Their ability to work and love was not born in the analysis but was a temporarily derailed function of a strong ego anchored in perhaps too harsh a superego. Otherwise they could not have made use of the transference, nor could they have traversed the separation from me as fully.

Chapter 6
False Claims of Incest

With incest-victim support groups forming everywhere and the public becoming sensitized to the existence of incest, it is not surprising that a number of patients present themselves with the belief or suspicion that this form of abuse has been their fate. Starting analytic therapy from such a premise creates a very different atmosphere, and dynamic, in the analytic dyad from the one I have discussed so far. Raphling (1994) has warned that

> an analyst's theory of pathogenesis accounts for a readiness to accept a patient's explanatory thesis at face value or to oppose it as contrary to the analyst's valued explanations. This mutual interest of analyst and patient in the pathogenic significance of sexual abuse can conspire to become a shared resistance to analysis of the defensive and gratifying aspects of pathology that remain hidden behind their conviction that a patient has been traumatized [p. 76].

I quite agree. But this powerful statement takes into consideration only the unexamined countertransference of the analyst. But as I have shown in the preceding chapters, awareness of countertransference plays a strong role in differentiating what is going on in the patient's psychic economy. I can only reiterate that a psychoanalysis is not an intellectual feat of piecing together a puzzle, but the active intellectual and emotional participation of two people in the search for maximum, but always relative, inner freedom from the distortions caused by past experience. That the analyst is more experienced than the patient, and therefore more flexible during this work, goes without saying. This flexibility, in my opinion, includes being able to overcome temporarily one's theoretical convictions to the extent that such openness will serve the analysand.

Laufer (1994) makes another observation. In the case of a young girl who was convinced that she had been sexually abused by her father, he recognized this allegation as delusional because "If she had actually been sexually abused by her father as a child, it would have been impossible for her to experience climax during intercourse because intercourse for sexually abused patients means a violent rape and a near-destruction of the oedipal parent" (p. 218).

I do not share Laufer's conviction that orgasm is an indicator of whether or not sexual abuse has taken place. Some patients are orgasmic while sadomasochistically fixated on traumatic events or sadistic objects and become temporarily frigid while the trauma is being worked through. Yet it would have been useful if the situation had been as clear cut in the cases of Annie Laviza and Allan Richmond. Both presented themselves for treatment in the firm belief that they had been the object of incest. They used this belief to excuse and explain any number of untoward events in their lives, including the clear wish for revenge and the assumption that, as victims, they were entitled to compensation by life, by analysis, by the whole world. In short, they showed all the hallmarks of being "the exceptions" to the rest of humanity that Freud described in 1916. Further, there was every indication that, like Shengold's (1991) patients, they had been overindulged by parents who did not know how to set boundaries.

ANNIE LAVIZA

Ms. Laviza came for treatment because she could not maintain a relationship with Terry, the only man whom she had ever loved. She traced this inability to incestuous abuse by her father from the time she was about six or seven years old until she began to menstruate. She was also very angry with her mother, whom she characterized as having "indulged her father's flamboyance." Father had died some years earlier when Ms. Laviza was in college. Mother had rapidly remarried. Ms. Laviza did not like the man and rebuffed his and her mother's many invitations. She preferred to meet her mother in restaurants or, on rare occasions, in her apartment, although, actually, she preferred her mother not to come to her apartment. She had bought it herself with money she inherited after father's death and felt it would somehow be less her own if mother came too often. Ms. Laviza despised her mother for being "a dishrag" when it came to indulging her husbands, relatives, and friends Apparently, the woman was unable to say "no" to demands for money, time, or gifts.

Ms. Laviza characterized herself as a kind and giving person who was often misunderstood and misused by her friends, both male and female. She supposed that this behavior was somehow linked to the abuse by her father; she did not know how. She did not think of herself as a dishrag like her mother, she added, more like a doormat She thought this remark enormously witty. The defensive aspect of this humor was not at all apparent to her. In her rather high-level computer job she also felt misused and unappreciated. The only place outside of her apartment where she really felt safe was her fitness club. There she was admired for her stamina and form and received the praise she felt she deserved everywhere. She made it clear that she expected similar praise from me, "to make up for what I missed out on." She didn't care what my fee was because she knew that analytic training was long and expensive and "you always get what you pay for." A very low-cost analyst would not suit her, she felt, because such an analyst would be inferior. Rather than engaging her in prolonged discussion about fees and schedules, I suggested a trial period of three months. Lauding me for my caution, she readily agreed.

> Not another one! I have the hours, but do I have the strength for another narcissist? She looked like a mouse peering in at me through the half-opened door and then marching in like the Prussian army. . . . The two sides of the narcissist revealed at once. One session and she reminds me of M., needing to be shored up; only you can't shore her up because she is like a bottomless pit. So, given that she does remind me of M., is taking her on a *Wiedergutmachen* [undoing] or a genuine wish to help her? Time will tell.

The Beginning

The initial phase of Ms. Laviza's analytic therapy resembled the proverbial honeymoon. Ms. Laviza felt unaccountably joyful and claimed that for the first time in years she could face her problems without undue anxiety. She did not even mind the difficulties with her beloved Terry as much. Terry wanted to see other women but remain on friendly terms with his

Annie. Ms. Laviza felt hurt, bewildered, and wounded but did not dare to complain for fear of losing him altogether. She had discussed this turn of events with each of her girlfriends until they now avoided her or met her only if she promised not to talk about Terry. Her mother, usually a willing listener, also appeared bored by her compulsive repetition and examination of every word Terry had spoken and every glance he might or might not have thrown in her direction. Because she had "unconditionally accepted his terms," he called her frequently to ask for small favors or advice. In return, he took her out to lunch or met her for a movie. Ms. Laviza felt terribly misused but unable to shed her obsession with him. No other man interested her, nor did any other subject. She felt deeply indebted to me because she was certain that without my listening to her constant worrying and obsessing she would "make a mistake and let him know how I really feel." She feared that if she ever confronted Terry with her woundedness, he would never speak with her again and that would be "the death of me." Life without Terry would be insufferable. She divided her free time into segments spent either working out at her club or talking about Terry during her sessions, followed by lonely hours waiting for the phone to ring or spending much care on running some errand for Terry.

When our three-month trial time came to an end, she "could not think of leaving you any more than I can think of leaving Terry." She proved what she meant by sitting in the waiting room until the last of my patients had left and I prepared to go home. She apologized for her transgression, assuring me "that it will never happen again." In subsequent sessions she did not permit examination of the suspicion, need for control, and lack of self-esteem displayed in this act. Instead, she seemed rather pleased with her determination to show me how much she valued me.

> No wonder Terry wants to run. I feel myself absolutely enraged and choked. So what could have happened to this lady? What makes her so desperate? There is something almost psychotic behind this iron determination to have what she wants when she wants it. Where does all that submissive, passive-aggressive clinging come from. Not that she can associate . . . . I am overlooking something here. There must be something powerful and hateful in her, or does she think her vagina is defective and therefore destructive and has driven Terry away, and because she is so

defective she must now be a good girl and do his—and my—bidding by doing his errands and by being an outwardly compliant patient for me? I experience her as a tension producing bore who wants to cling and choke.

Recollections

As the analysis unfolded, little windows opened in the unending narrative about Terry. Ms. Laviza became able to hear occasional comments I made when I inquired about how she felt about taking Terry's suit to the cleaner or what went through her mind when Terry spent the weekend with a new girlfriend after having promised to take her to the movies. She took these questions as proof that I was interested in her and would not fail her "when I really need you." At this point, she felt she did not really need me but that my daily presence was comforting nevertheless. In her own way, she appeared to idealize me as a nonperson who was of great importance only insofar as I was able to make her feel whole, or so she claimed.

The weekend separations were experienced as grave insults. When once again I pointed out that she seemed to believe that I could not remember her during the weekend, as she feared Terry did not remember her, she settled down to tell me more about her background. She had always adored her father, whose favorite she was. Therefore, nobody thought it strange that she was permitted in the parental bedroom. The parents slept in separate beds, and mother was aware that little Annie crawled in bed with father. Much to her surprise, she also recalled that mother did not allow her to stay in father's bed but insisted that she come to her. Puzzled by this recollection, she checked it with her mother, who launched into a laughing retelling of Annie's exploits as a young child. Apparently both parents found her delightful but had no patience with her. They both worked in the father's business. Annie was taken care of by a series of baby sitters. Ms. Laviza was puzzled by all of this. If mother had always been there when she was in father's bed, how could he have abused her? She soon found an answer. It had all taken place under the blanket, so mother couldn't tell what was going on. And a good thing, too, according to Ms. Laviza, because, with mother's insistence that she occupy mother's rather than father's bed, she might have turned into a Lesbian!

Up to this point, Ms. Laviza had interpreted my silences and occasional interpretive questions as silent approval. Now she became angry and accused me of being like Terry, the deserter. Terry had given her a gold bracelet for her birthday, but she felt like throwing it at his feet or, better yet, stuffing it in his mouth. She hoped he would choke on it. But, of course, she had said nothing. Just as I never said anything, thereby neglecting her. I tried to draw a parallel for her between wanting to choke Terry and what she felt in the transference. She was incensed. How could I possibly think that I could ever be as important or as beloved as Terry? She stormed out of the office, still highly indignant at the end of the session.

But the reactivation of her grandiose self (Kohut, 1977) did not protect her for very long. Hypochondriacal concerns began to trouble her. When she was not talking about Terry, she was discussing the size and color of her feces, her menstrual blood, and the possibility that she would be unable to have children with anyone besides Terry. She suffered many head colds. There were large secondary gains involved for her in appearing ill. Mother would come over with soup and good advice, and even Terry became more attentive. After one bout with a cough that "almost turned into pneumonia," Terry agreed to stay overnight. They cuddled under the blanket but "nothing happened." Nevertheless, Ms. Laviza's hopes were rekindled.

The similarity between climbing into father's bed and cuddling with Terry under a blanket became apparent to her. She angrily asked me if I thought that she wanted to come and sit on my lap because, if so, she wanted to "disabuse me of this notion." Again, she claimed that her father had abused her. I interpreted that perhaps she felt abused here, during sessions, because I did not ask her to sit on my lap. Crying silently, she proceeded to tell me about her father. This took many sessions. Apparently, he had been a handsome man who favored lots of gold jewelry and expensive suits. He had "fancied the ladies and they fancied him but he had high blood pressure and so he stayed faithful to my mother even when he did not want to be faithful" was the first version. When he was at home, he played with Annie and showered her with expensive gifts, a habit he never lost. Annie had everything material her heart could desire. To this day, she has always owned the best, newest, and most expensive of any new fad or fashion as father had taught her.

Before meeting Terry, she was involved with a "dreadful man whom I loved to pieces" but who turned out to be a gigolo. He took her money and was sweet but never repaid loans. In the end, he laughed at her and ran off to Atlantic City with a "bimbo." Her mother had warned her, but she had been helpless in the throes of her passion for this man. Now she was ashamed of the episode but also proud that she had been able to buy such a charming man. Intellectually, she understood that this part of her life, which had taken up the better part of five years, was a repetition of her mother's fate with her father. But this understanding did not help her to draw any parallels to her present, equally compulsive behavior with Terry. It had dawned on her that there might be a connection between all this and her past so that she was now willing to speak about her childhood.

Across the street from the family's home lived a good friend of her mother's, Irene, who ran a business similar to the parents'. "They were always in each other's house. We all ran in and out of each other's rooms and were like one family. They were always teasing each other about each other's sex life, and my mother and I thought it was all just a joke." This constituted the second version of her family myth. Much later, during highly charged sessions that began with tales of Terry's obnoxious behavior and faithlessness, a third version emerged. This version remained and was substantiated in dreams and corroborated by mother. During a visit with Irene, "my father died in her bed. He had on all of his jewelry and nothing else. Irene called my mother to come and get him. But he was dead. A stroke. They all said, 'What a beautiful death. What a way to go.' I hate him. I hate them all."

After this dramatic disclosure, Terry was no longer the focus of her longing. Although Ms. Laviza would not admit for a long time that he had been a surrogate for her unfaithful father, she became able to examine more closely the many empathic failures she had experienced in her childhood and adolescence. Intrigued and seduced by the glamour and excitement surrounding her father, little Annie had been his most fervent admirer. She followed him around whenever she could, and he tolerated her presence. But she was also her mother's ally.

154 ♦ Chapter 6

Mother knew what her husband and alleged friend were up to. To verify her suspicions, she sent the child across the street with offerings of cake or fruit. Ms. Laviza remembered how often she had to ring the bell before it was answered and how often mother sent her back when there was no answer at all. "I know they are in there. Go find them for me." She also recalled the feeling states of these humiliating and frightening experiences. "It didn't get better when I grew up. If anything, it got worse. Mother would make me stand behind the house in the bushes and spy on them. Or she had me follow them in my new car so she could go and scream at them. Only she never screamed; she just threatened my father that she would throw him out and never allow him to see me again."

Little Annie, and now the grown-up Ms. Laviza, came to see herself as the person who held father, as the person who was his true love because her very presence was enough to keep him at home on the many occasions when mother tried to prevent him from "going across the street." She defensively believed herself to be the only female he loved and therefore the only one who could control him into staying home. This belief was reinforced by both her parents; by the mother who needed to use the child as an extension of her jealous rages and to control her husband, and by the father, who seemed genuinely fond of the little girl but had no idea how to treat children. He bought her off with gifts and by "wheedling" when he wanted to be rid of her. Wheedling meant that he kissed and hugged her, pinched her bottom, and stuck money into her hand. "I thought I was pretty," she reported bitterly. "He told me I was and I believed it until I hit high school and nobody would date me." It took a good deal longer until she realized that the reason for there being no dates was quite different from what she thought: she was so intent on following father, on finding out what he was up to, that she was rarely, if ever, available for interaction with her peers.

Her contempt for the other teenagers grew in proportion to her involvement with her parents' drama. Her peers seemed unenlightened and stupid to her, now the center of an ongoing saga of unfulfilled love and betrayal. The car she used to follow her father and his mistress had been a gift from him. She felt disloyal to him but also furious that he had betrayed her as well as her mother. No longer able to feel herself his favorite, she had to admit to the shame and humiliation of being left out in the cold, both figuratively and literally. It was a bitter day for her when she was able to admit to herself that far from being father's sexual partner, she had been a frustrated spy in the service of her mother. Worst of all, she blamed herself for her father's death. By then a young adult, she had begun to refuse to do her mother's bidding. She was amazed when I interpreted this behavior as a healthy attempt to separate and lead her own life. On the contrary, "It was probably my fault the son of a bitch died then. If I had been watching them like I used to, I might have realized his blood pressure was high and stopped him from going across the street," she said.

When this material came to light, Ms. Laviza began to report dreams that reflected what she spoke about. The stilted way of talking and lack of associative material gave way to an emotional and unaffected way of reporting and associating. Nevertheless, during this time, the analysis was in serious danger. Ms. Laviza could barely stand the humiliation and deflation of her grandiosity. In the transference, she experienced me primarily as the elusive, seductive father. Thus, I seemed dangerous and uncontrollable to her. At other times she could barely tolerate being in the same room with me when I in some way reminded her of Irene, the secret lover. She had to sit up and look at me in order to ascertain that I had not been transformed into the hated rival. Worst of all for her were the times when she saw me as the mother who had used her for her own purposes. As a result of the tension built within the sessions, her work at the fitness club became even more compulsive. There she released her fury in frenzied physical activity.

When she was nearly suicidal with impotent rage and shame, I used the words "detective work" to describe the activities she had undertaken on behalf of her mother. She felt oddly relieved by this description. She had thought of herself as a spy who could not be forgiven. I used this opening to point out that she could hardly have been expected to deal all by herself with the many primal scenes she must have witnessed. I also acknowledged as understandable her outrage at being used as an executive tool of her mother's will. It then became possible for Ms. Laviza to understand that she had created the fantasy of being father's mistress in order to deal with her oedipal longing and to defend herself against the overstimulation of being forced to witness the many primal scenes. Ms. Laviza could give up responsibility for her incestuous arousal and preserve the image of her mother as good and caring for her daughter as long as she fantasized father as being an abuser. Being betrayed and a victim along with mother also allowed her to stay identified with the maternal good-enough object despite the fact that mother was so taken up with her own defeat that she was not able to help her daughter traverse the oedipal phase. Instead, the little girl, and later the teenager, was overstimulated by being made part of both parents' sexual longings. Rather than mourning father's desertion and, later, his death, she kept him alive by accusing him of having abused her sexually.

After five years in treatment, Ms. Laviza left, having changed her career. She had become part-owner of a fitness club where she had no difficulty in meeting and dating men. She triumphantly showed me a picture of a handsome muscle builder who had become her fiancée. Terry had remained a constant friend. There had been a reconciliation of sorts with mother and stepfather as well, though Ms. Laviza remained suspicious of her mother's motives.

DISCUSSION

Ms. Laviza's analysis was marked by repeated swings between idealizing me and denigrating me in the transference. The reactivation of her grandiose self during treatment showed itself sometimes in haughty demandingness, at other times in almost groveling admiration in the transference. I imagine that as a child she must have been overcome by loneliness and frustration at being used without empathy by both parents for their own ends. There seems to have been little or no regard for the growing child's developmental needs, nor any attempts to understand her age-appropriate longing. Shame and humiliation accompanied her every memory, the major part of her inner life taken up with defending herself against overstimulation, frustration, and oedipal longings. She defensively created the myth of an incestuous father in order to feel special and loved at all. The fantasy allowed her to think of herself as a victim who had been wronged but who was not responsible for her delusional oedipal victory. The process of understanding how the past was influencing her present helped her to acknowledge the defensive nature of her fantasy.

At first, she repeated her oedipal scenario with Terry. As the transference deepened, she began to wrestle with almost unbearable states of shame and humiliation caused by being used without regard for her own needs. She first became hypochondriacal, then suicidal in an effort not to know the truth. The fantasy of being an incest victim had allowed her to build a false persona whereby she was entitled to reparation and special treatment by one and all. In contrast to her self-inflating fantasy, she recreated the humiliation and self-denigration of her traumatic involvement with her parents' faithlessness in her own relationships. The obsessiveness of these relationships stemmed from a lack of tension release and the impossibility of escaping the repetition compulsion.

Despite such splitting, denial, and disavowal, Ms. Laviza could care deeply for another person. Her relationship with Terry survived many upheavals. Both found different sexual partners but stayed devoted to each other as friends. This might seem surprising in view of her generally narcissistic self-organization, but, from the beginning of the analysis, she was able to use an idealizing transference to keep herself from totally floundering. I hypothesized that in her infancy her mother had cared for her appropriately and that her father's delight in her infantile exploits had allowed her to form the beginning of a cohesive self. Therefore, she did not sink altogether into the quagmire of narcissistic rage and helplessness. During the prolonged working-through period, she began to be open to empathic comments that at first did not include reconstructions. Later, she was able to reflect on the defensive nature of her oedipal fantasy and to mourn her father and her childhood.

There was a marked absence of dreams in the opening phase of her analysis. Concomitant with the lifting of repression and the appearance of memories, delusional fantasies of having been incestuously abused dissolved. Body language and motility were communicative and self-satisfying aspects of her ego. These functions were not instinctualized but were used in the service of conscious abreaction without regression (Siegel, 1984, 1991; Siegel et al., 1996). When regression did occur it was confined to the sessions, indicating a less splintered ego than might have been expected.

ALLAN RICHMOND

Mr. Richmond thought that he really did not need an analyst. It was merely curiosity on his part that prompted him to present himself for analysis. His interest was aroused because he had seen such good results when a friend and colleague had obtained "truly enviable results" in his treatment. However, this friend did not wish to pass on the name of his analyst because that might interfere both with his analysis and their friendship. Therefore, Mr. Richmond had come to me, although he thought it laughable that his friend was so jealous of his therapist. He had obtained my name from his wife, who had heard me lecture. She was very much in favor of his treatment because lately there had been grave difficulties in their marriage. She hoped that her husband would "shape up" in an analysis. They both wanted a child, but because his wife expected him to come home each evening with "a raging erection" he felt resentful and was unwilling to have intercourse.

He was at a loss to explain why his interest in his wife had waned. He thought it had to do with "sex on demand" when making a baby. His wife had decided to ascertain her fertile time by taking her temperature daily. This procedure seemed repugnant to Mr. Richmond, especially because they had both been assured that there was no physical problem. He hoped time would heal whatever it was that kept his wife from becoming pregnant. He did not believe that either he or his wife had any psychological problem severe enough to hinder conception. His marriage was important to him. He saw his wife as his anchor in reality because he had no head for business and let his wife manage his business affairs.

He described himself as a man who often reflected on his behavior and was careful "to pull my weight in the world." He was a musician who was a performer, teacher, and aspiring composer. He had won a bit of acclaim and was very much smitten with the idea of becoming famous. His wife resented the many hours he had to spend with publicity people and with rehearsing. He suspected that the idea of having a baby now was her way of holding on to him even more tightly than before. Claiming to be and to have been an exemplary husband, he professed not to know why she was so insecure about their relationship. Some of his compositions were also becoming known, and he felt that he was "pregnant" with an ambitious undertaking. He wanted to write a work around Orpheus from a different point of view. A recurring dream had "put me on the track" of doing so. He had begun to compose but found himself blocked. Up to this point in his life he had always been productive and creative. His analyzing friend had told him that he might be competing with his wife about who could create what first. This thought had shaken him sufficiently to follow his wife's suggestion that he enter analysis. And, oh yes, by the way, he had been seduced by his mother when he became able to "hold an erection" at about 10 or 12 years of age.

Quite satisfied with this parting shot, he left before we could discuss schedules and the usual arrangements. Such cliffhangers became part and parcel of his analysis. He was aware that this behavior produced unease in most people and agreed that it was designed as a manipulation. He did not wish to discuss my fee because this would influence him negatively in relation to me. Being aware that he had to pay for his sessions would make him feel like a consumer, and he despised consumers. He believed in "the simple life" of eating organically grown vegetables and meat that had not been tampered with by hormones. He grew a few tomatoes and cucumbers himself and regretted that he did not have more time to garden.

So far, he claimed, he agreed with almost anything I had said. But this did not mean that agreement prompted a change in his thinking or behavior. To him, agreeing simply meant that "I take into consideration what other people think and do." But this consideration did not include a wish to incorporate other people's opinions or wishes into his own actions. He wanted to be "my own man," uninfluenced by anyone. He prided himself on being intuitive and gentle. Not being particularly good looking, he nevertheless managed to draw attention to himself by graceful, somewhat effete gesticulation and colorful clothing. When he entered analysis, he favored American Indian jewelry, jeans, and denim shirts. This style was not at all in vogue then, so that people were drawn to his exotic exterior and asked him questions about his apparel. He liked this attention very much, whereas his wife dreaded it. He could not understand her feeling at all because they had met for the same reason that other people sought his company. She had interviewed him for a small-town newspaper before he became known and had picked him out of a crowd of contestants at a competition as much for his attire as for his performance.

Reluctant to marry anyone, he had succumbed to his wife's invitation to marry because from the beginning she had protected him by keeping unwanted admirers away. She accompanied him on every tour. Lately, he had begun to resent her fierce loyalty because it kept him "shackled" to her. He wished she would stay home and let him go on the road by himself. But she wouldn't hear of it. After many sessions of talking around the subject, he finally told me that he liked to go to the saunas that were located in public baths visited by homosexuals. What amused and aroused him there was that seeing so many naked men prancing around reminded him of his mother. While looking at the men around him, he fantasized about her body. He was sad that she, now in her mid-70s, had pendulous breasts and wrinkles and was no longer the radiant beauty he remembered. After having been with such a "fine woman," he could not possibly entertain any homosexual fantasies or wishes, he maintained.

It became clear that to a certain extent he identified with his mother. He mourned her fading beauty as much as she did. Mother had had several face lifts and was "still scrumptious," but he was no longer seduced by her. She was too old. The moral implications of desiring one's mother as an adult seemed to elude him. His wife and his mother did not get along with each other, each wanting to be the center of his attention. But the center of his life was his music, he stated, and there was no room for the selfish needs of anyone else. He felt drained by both his mother and his wife. As a matter of fact, he believed that artists should stay away from any commitment to people. They ideally should be able to "walk their splendid road in splendid isolation." In particular the composition named Orpheus had become his focus of attention. When I asked who might be the Eurydice to his Orpheus, he became vague. What interested him was not the woman involved but the journey into Hades and the music Orpheus played on his harp.

It took some time before he revealed the recurring dream that had so inspired him. He was not yet ready to talk about his recurring dream, but did talk about current dreams. The first one he brought in, after eight months of treatment, follows: A blond tiger stalks up and down in a familiar room and growls and shows his teeth. At first he is afraid of it, but then he strokes its fur, and it turns into a blond poodle with which he plays. In his associations, the familiar room turned out to be my treatment room, and I was cast as the tiger/poodle. He found this imagery highly entertaining, stating that he always had sexual intercourse with the people he really became close to and that he found it interesting that here, in my presence, there was such a clear boundary. With a high-pitched laugh, he said, "I wouldn't mind trying to cross that border." I asked him whom these thoughts reminded him of and he replied, "My beautiful mother, of course. You couldn't be bitchy like my wife, and you wouldn't always expect me to have an erection when I didn't feel like it." I agreed with him that it is tiresome to be expected to be potent every night, but how was it that he saw me as less than human, namely, a tiger or a poodle? He was not at a loss for words. He saw me as a tiger because he could "sense" that I had considerable power, and as a poodle I was, to him, adorable. Besides, he liked animals better than people. He became euphoric after these declarations, entirely satisfied that he had plumbed the depth of his transference.

So why does this man not elicit sympathy from me, let alone empathy? He's hysterical, self-serving, narcissistic, full of distortions and projections. If he is so identified with mother, he really should be homosexual, yet he denies the possibility of even a fantasy about men. If he had disidentified from mother, as he should have, he wouldn't have so much trouble with his wife. As it is, she is the one who has my sympathy. Imagine living with a guy who only notices his own problems! Wish he'd tell me the recurrent dream that inspired his Orpheus opus-to-be. He openly invites me to castrate him—"You wouldn't expect me to have an erection"—and castrates me by declaring me to be an animal. Yet he finds me exciting as a tiger (who'll bite his head/penis off) and adorable as a poodle (when he has masturbatory urges), stroking me, his new baby penis. So I seem to be his new selfobject, a role I do not relish. Yet he is creative, maybe even capable of sublimation. Probably instinctualizes all over the place, but I don't feel it. When he throws eroticism around, I find him vaguely infantile, no response to being courted . . . . he just seems in denial. Supposing he sees all women as having a penis; then all that sleeping around would be homosexual in nature, he, with his baby penis, seducing women whom he imagines as having a phallus. I guess he glued one on me also. And that is what makes me uneasy. Or are there hidden fantasies of becoming female? Maybe he styles himself Eurydice rather than Orpheus . . . .

Recollections

Mr. Richmond's life history did not emerge gradually but burst forth with great urgency when he, or I, least expected it. He was much preoccupied with the ever-shifting transference. He had read all of Freud's recommendations for treatment and scrutinized my behavior for correctness against this standard. For instance, he discoursed on the permissibility of a hand-shake, allowed in Europe owing to societal norms but not in the U.S.A. He was intrigued by such differences and specu-lated how they would affect an analysis. On the other hand, he wanted me to break the rules and come to his performances. He was much irked by the as-if quality of the analysis and often told me that he by himself could do as much analyzing as I did. He expected an interpretation each hour, not once a month or so.

I tried to explore with him why my silences were such a threat. This question led to many dreams, all featuring fire and poles or ruins of poles. The most significant of them follows: It is Easter. There is a pole, and he is tied to it. He has to be tied like this so his family can have an Easter service. But the cross-bar cracks and he can get down. His father has been watching from afar and will build a new cross for him. His mother stands in the distance, quietly burning. He associatively identified the cross as his genitals and the fire as his mother's sexuality. According to him, the sexual act for men was a "cold and icy thing, not warm and creative as a uterus makes a woman." It became clear that he was envious of women's ability to bear children. He spent many sessions wrestling with this fantasy while his relationship with his wife deteriorated further. The more he withdrew from her, the more she pressed him for his emotional presence. She refused to go on tour with him, and this filled him with panic. When she was along, he refrained from going to the baths and did not have to deal with fans. How was he going to manage? He recognized that he had become dependent on his wife as he had been dependent on his mother.

To his horror, he became aware that he also felt tied to me. "But you wouldn't tie me to any cross, would you?" he pleaded. The magic quality he attached to his religious belief now came to the fore. Although he styled himself an atheist, he had been deeply influenced by Christian myths and beliefs. The cross as a place of martyrdom came up time and again. At first he was unable to see that being tied to the cross was not only a grandiose identification with the son of God, therefore making him godlike, but also contained what he was later to call "delicious pain." Before recognizing his sadomasochistic propensities, he defensively became hypochondriacal. He reported symptoms ranging from a heart murmur to cancer. He did not practice his instrument and avoided going to rehearsal with his band because the close proximity of sweating bodies repelled him. He clung to his wife, who nurtured his imaginary ills by bringing him breakfast in bed and rubbing his aching limbs with liniments. He was sure he had carpal tunnel syndrome and spent a lot of time running from one doctor to another. The dream of being tied to the cross of his family recurred in a slightly different version. This time, he put mother's fire out. "See?" he triumphed. "She made me sleep with her." He denied having any pleasurable feelings connected to rescuing his mother and warded off an interpretation of his oedipal conflict. I responded by telling him as gently and as offhandedly as I could that most of the time dreamers represent aspects of themselves in their dreams. He vehemently protested that he had no part in the seduction by the oedipal mother, insisting that she, not he, had "done the deed" of incest.

There is something entirely wrong with my perceptual system if that man has experienced incest. None of my usual responding symptoms are present. Maybe I need another analysis? I think he's talking of womb envy and of identification with his mother in an Oedipus complex that has gone sour. His genitals are the cross he has to bear and are not the source of pride and procreation as in other males. And, of course, he is Jesus Christ himself, the second coming. No doubt his mother spoiled him rotten, but I would bet she did not sleep with him. Still hasn't told me the Orpheus dream. He is a homosexual who wants to stay in the closet. Yes, no? Maybe I'll have a consultation with S.

More Recollections

Mr. Richmond's booking agent presented him with a schedule for his next tour. He immediately became panic stricken. Even if he could talk his wife into accompanying him, what about his schedule with me? He couldn't bear the separation at this point. And, besides, he was working on Orpheus, so how could he leave? He didn't feel like having sex with his wife. He felt like "fistfucking" her. He was not sure if that meant he wanted to penetrate her anus or her vagina. Taking pity on him, his wife agreed to go along on the tour. Strangely to him, this did reassure him. During the last session before leaving, he told me that he would call me often, try to have sessions over the phone if he was too distraught, and also write to me. I had not heard from him for four months when he returned, assuming that I had kept his sessions open for him. Although the tour had been successful, he was "in bad shape." They had passed through his hometown where he and his wife had visited his parents. Mother, "siding with my wife," had exhorted him to produce grandchildren for her. He tried to hug his father, who repulsed him by making sure their hands met in a handshake "somewhere in the vicinity of their belly buttons." He managed to hug father after all, and it was "like hugging a truck." He felt no response and wondered if his mother had to put up with such unresponsiveness as well. If so, he could begin to understand why she had turned to him.

Because father had always been a loner and shunned social events, mother had taken little Allan with her to parties, shopping, and to concerts, where he learned early to sit still and to listen. Because he soon began to like being mother's constant companion and made precocious remarks about musicians, mother talked father into letting him take instrumental lessons. Father was not pleased that his son wanted to enter "the hungry life of a musician" but relented when he was told that the child had talent. Later, father gloried in the early success his son had as a performer; he clipped reviews from newspapers and at receptions for the young prodigy drew attention to his parental self. As Mr. Richmond put it, "He was interested in my product, not in me." Deeply disappointed in his father during these teen years, he turned to mother for emotional support. But she was smitten with the glamour her son had brought into her life and instead of sharing his emotional concerns pushed him to accept as many bookings as he could. He felt like a "zombie who could produce music." As soon as he could reasonably do so, he left home and went to college. There he encountered musicians who introduced him to other forms of music. He discontinued training as a performer and dedicated himself to composition.

Both parents were upset and refused to speak with him for years. Because he had earned enough money previously, he was independent of the disappointed and disappointing parents. As far as he was concerned, there wasn't any need to contact them at all. He began to introduce his own compositions, formed a band, and again earned money as a performer. It was on a performing tour that he met his wife.

After discussing the earlier events in detail, he described a sexual foursome his wife had arranged. He was very much repelled by the other man in his bed, enjoyed making love to the other woman, but felt like killing the stranger's husband when he had intercourse with his wife. When the man turned to him for anal intercourse, he at first liked the idea but then became nauseated at the thought of being penetrated in this fashion. He clearly wanted me to praise him for his feelings of repugnance. While I was still weighing my thoughts about how to deal with this event and questioning silently if there had not been some collaboration in the arrangements on Mr. Richmond's part, he announced that he had decided to divorce his wife. He found her behavior perverse and would have none of it in the future. Of course, he made his pronouncement as he was leaving, so I could not respond to it. Aware that he did not want me to respond, I said nothing about his announcement when he came the next day. He had indeed gone home to tell his wife of his intentions. She was horrified and begged him to reconsider. When Mr. Richmond left, I found a call from his wife on the answering machine. She blamed me for her husband's decision to divorce her and wanted to have sessions in conjunction with her husband. He was curious on the following day: Would I see them as a couple? I declined, telling him that there were many reasons why I could not do that, the most important being that it would interrupt his analysis. He was nonplussed by this answer and spent the whole session ruminating about my refusal. He had been free of hypochondriacal preoccupations for some time, linking the symptom removal to the fact that he could speak freely in his analysis and to my letting him "go on tour without hounding me." He now was certain that his wife, like his mother, was only interested in his ability to hold an erection. He derided himself for thinking that his wife "was the holder of his sexuality." He had been able to satisfy many women; she was not "the only vessel into which he could pour himself."

During this time of hauteur and pseudo-self-sufficiency, he became particularly adept in the use of cliff hangers. He would spend a session rummaging around on the couch, complaining about the temperature in the room, discussing what he thought he knew of my life, and then, suddenly, at the end of the hour, tell me a dream and throw me a bit of information about the progress of his divorce proceedings. It never occurred to him to suggest analysis or any form of counseling for his wife. I finally asked him how it was that the woman who had for so long been the only female he trusted had suddenly become so distasteful to him. He seemed to care nothing for her. He didn't see it that way. She had tried to "sap my energy even further by introducing me to lewd behavior."

My interpretive inquiry opened the door for a displaced negative transference to enter the analysis. The counterphobic aspects of the unfulfilled sexual encounter with his wife's lover and the fear of being drained now were firmly placed on my shoulders. But while berating me and my profession, he also began to feel better. The absence of expected retribution during the sessions allowed him to feel safe enough to confront the issues that had clouded his life. He no longer feared being seduced by me or anyone else but felt that he could handle anyone who tried to drain (i.e., seduce) him. He finally told me the dream that had inspired him to begin writing new music to the myth of Orpheus. In it, he is in a Mexican landscape confronted by an ancient pueblo. There is a very small opening leading to a magnificent proscenium hewn out of rock. He climbs down and then up many stairs in search of a melody. A beautiful old Mexican lady hands him a lyre and says, "Sing." He associated to this dream that if he had dreamed it for the first time while in analysis, he "would have sworn the old Mexican was my analyst, but now I believe it to be either my wife or my mother." His was puzzled about the fact that these two women, whom he now saw as dangerous and draining, appeared also to be his muses. He began to understand the dream differently when finally his incest fantasy dissolved. But first, during his endeavor to construct a new inner world, he was able to examine his relationship with his parents. Shocked to discover that he treated his wife as unempathically as his father had treated him and his mother, he began to admit his attraction to men. One of the musicians who regularly traveled with him on tour was the object of his affections. But this man was not interested in anyone who was married. Mr. Richmond suffered all the pain of unrequited love.

The abrupt way of throwing a piece of information at me on leaving decreased. Genuinely afraid that I would stop him from a homosexual encounter, he wondered why I did not interfere. I pointed out that we still did not know the origins or the functions of his aggression toward his wife. He had forgotten that he once wished to penetrate her with his fist, he said, but what I said seemed true. It now seemed to him that he wanted to be the recipient of anal penetration and no longer had the desire to enter his wife in this fashion. He wondered if it was even possible to stick one's whole fist into another person's anus without inflicting pain. Sadistic fantasies of castrating women now began to plague him. He dreamed of crosses again, but this time he was the executioner who bound the women to the cross and tortured them by stroking their vaginas and breasts. The musician seemed less attractive to him, but so did his wife. She had prolonged divorce proceedings and was still in the same house with him. She still had not given up. But he could not tolerate coming near her for fear of hurting her or of acting out his fantasy.

While still struggling to understand this split-off part of himself, he had another dream in which he was sitting on the lap of an old Indian, smoking a peace pipe. But while making peace, he held the man's testicles in his hand and discovered them to be like slimy, moldering mushrooms. He shuddered when he reported this dream. After acknowledging that the shudder also felt "delicious," he recovered memories of going to camp at a very early age. He had begged to be sent there. His parents did not want him to go so far away, but he had insisted because an admired older cousin spent each summer there. He was the youngest boy at this camp and often unable to keep up with the demanding schedule. When the group he was assigned to went on long hikes in the mountains, he often had to stay behind in the care of one of the counselors. He cried and screamed, but this tactic, so successful with his parents, did not work there. The counselors just ignored him until he quieted down and then, when he behaved himself, as a reward told him stories of the old West.

Mr. Richmond immediately had a suspicion that it was these counselors, not his mother, who had seduced him. Slowly, we began to reconstruct what must have happened. Allan had not counted on being lonely or homesick. It was also the first time that he was not the center of attention and the first time he did not excel in any and all endeavors. In particular, he missed the lavish praise of his mother. He remembered that he was incensed that she had let him go to the camp although he had fervently wished it. He drew the parallel to some of his trans-ference feelings when I did not give him advice. He felt unpro-tected and vulnerable not only while camping but also when he had to shower with all the other boys. They teased him about the undeveloped size of his genitals, sometimes pulling on them and telling him that he would never be able to "ride a woman." When he came home, he vowed to himself that he would "ride" the best and most lovable woman he knew, namely, his mother. But he found it difficult to act on his fantasy. Mother allowed him to kiss her on the cheek when he returned home and cheer-fully told him that big boys did not cling to their mothers. He was now a big boy who could go to camp all by himself. Allan had not expected such a reception. He had wanted to snuggle and to sit on his mother's lap, as he had done previously. Now, he had to separate psychologically from his beautiful mother when he was not at all ready for it. The reparative fantasies he used to compensate for the sudden loss of his excessively indulgent childhood mother accompanied him into adulthood. He suspected a seductive and castrating mother in every fe-male he met and expected each male friend to be as unap-proachable as his father had been. Mr. Richmond filled many sessions with tears, mourning his victim status. He gave in to his wife's pleas to try to rescue their marriage. To his great shame, he found himself impotent with her. He briefly thought of having a homosexual affair but did not act on it. Instead, he settled down to discover the origins of his impotence.

An interpretation that both his impotence with his wife and the desire to have a man as lover might be a flight from the transference enabled him to understand the see-saw of his libidinal investments. It had not been possible to identify with his father because this man was distant, even hostile. Mother found her son a more desirable companion than her husband and therefore did not permit psychological separation. To rescue himself from the incestuous pull of an overindulgent, needy mother, young Allan had fled into a defensive masculinity that was shored up by sadistic and grandiose fantasies of having possessed his mother sexually. His potency fully returned soon after he recognized that "mother was always on my back and didn't even know it." His wife was now seen as the executrix of his own perverse fantasies. A reconciliation took place when she agreed to present herself for analytic treatment. Mr. Richmond left his treatment after he had rescued his Eurydice.

Discussion

Mr. Richmond used his rich fantasy life to defend himself against his strong oedipal longing for his seductive, beautiful mother. In the effort to keep himself distanced and invulnerable to such seductions, he developed grandiose expectations and the need for perverse gratification. He became Christ on the cross. But his superego prevented the ecstasy he hoped for by, in fantasy, turning aggression against himself. The unresolved conflict between him and his parents made itself felt by producing impotence and allowing others to drain him by taking advantage of his contacts, his money, and, often, his body in promiscuous encounters. Being taken advantage of meant the inability to provide mother with a mature companion and aroused anxious expectation of punishment from a vengeful father. His task was to sexually fulfill both parents. Sadomasochistic submissiveness to casual lovers for a while relieved him of tension and castration fear. In sexual surrender to unknown women he could identify with his neglected mother and undo his castration fears. But sublimation in creative work eluded him. He was blocked. This block disappeared without our specifically analyzing it when he became aware of its function as a retaining wall against unreasonable demands by his family. When he felt particularly exploited, he counterphobically propelled himself into exhibitionistic and aggressive behaviors that made him feel invulnerable. But his inner structure included a strict superego. When both the repetition compulsion and the need to discharge tension could have been acted out in the tableau of two couples in simultaneous sexual intercourse, he felt nauseated and repulsed. His wife had become the fantasied incestuous mother from whom he tried to extract reparation. Hypochondriacal preoccupations served as a self-validating and self-protective device against retribution by internalized aggressive selfobjects. Because separation from his mother took place very late and in a forced, unempathic manner, he retained the introject of a phallic mother who could and would rob him of his penis.

In the transference he tested over and over again to see if revenge was forthcoming. Although I initially responded to him as if he were a narcissistic personality, I had to revise my opinion. He certainly had many narcissistic features, but, once we had worked through his exhibitionism, he revealed himself to be a person who could forgive transgression and love deeply. The coldness and rancor he had displayed toward his wife-as-incestuous-mother disappeared entirely once he had given up the need to control and manipulate her in order to stave off castration. His homosexual fantasies also served to ward off castration fears and enabled him defensively to hold on to exhibitionism and grandiose fantasies of having been an oedipal victor. During the beginning phase, he sexualized the transference in order to maintain control over murderous impulses toward his mother and the analyst-as-mother. He professed to have sex with anybody who became close to him. He felt relief when his attempt to destroy his mother imago was not countered by aggression, enabling him to allow homosexual fantasies to emerge. These homosexual fantasies were an attempt to gain the parental phallus that, he felt, his mother had robbed him of by possessing it herself. The almost delusional quality of his incest fantasy gave way when his sexual-identity confusion was dissolved, giving way to a consolidated, masculine ego. He became able to nurture his wife and to reassess his relationship with his needy mother.

SUMMARY

Ms. Laviza and Mr. Richmond both claimed that they had been sexually abused as children. This fantasy allowed them to stave off the disappointment of not being their opposite-sex parent's lover. Overindulged and ignored at the same time, they were, as children, assigned the task of healing parental wounds. They were incorporated by their parents as possessions without needs of their own. The ambiguous messages they received from their parents prevented them from fully understanding, enjoying, and accepting their own sexuality. After all, sometimes they were desperately needed by their parents, at other times ignored completely. Thus, overstimulation of their oedipal wishes did not allow them to separate fully at the age-appropriate time. They replayed in the transference their fear of being seduced by a parent and distrusted me for a long time. Mr. Richmond, in particular, hid under a cover of arrogance and manipulation in order to disavow his sadism and his castration fears. While there was some somatization of conflict in both analysands, this was not a stable feature of their psychic economy but a defensive reaction against emerging insight. Although their perception of reality was distorted, they did not regress deeply or dissociate. Their transferences were at times sexualized so that they experienced the analytic abstinence as painful and unfair, but they nevertheless were open to interpretation. In addition, my countertransference was devoid of the symptomology I experienced with analysands who had suffered incest. The reported transgression did not feel genuine to me but had a flat quality, which made me question the accuracy of the reports.

Epilogue

The symptoms most often associated with incestuous abuse and that guide psychoanalytic diagnostic assumptions include disturbance in reality testing; psychotic manifestations; dissociation; fear of seduction by the analyst; lack of trust in interpersonal relationships; panic attacks; somatization, including somatic memory; cognitive deficits, such as inability to concentrate or to remember; specific learning blocks; object-coercive doubting; symbolic enactment of conflict; motoric discharge patterns; and lack of orgasmic response (Kramer, 1983; Dewald, 1989; Levine, 1990; Laufer, 1994). While some or all of these symptoms can occur in a person who has experienced incest, I did not find that they reliably predict absence or presence of incestuous trauma in analysands. The distribution of symptoms among my group of incestuously abused patients is of interest:

disturbance of reality testing: 3
psychotic manifestations: 4
dissociation: 4
fear of seduction by the analyst: 4
lack of trust in interpersonal relationships: 6
panic attacks: 0
somatization including somatic memory: 5
cognitive deficits, such as inability to concentrate or to remember: 3
specific learning blocks: 1
object-coercive doubting: 3
symbolic enactment of conflict: 4
motoric discharge patterns: 6
lack of orgasmic response: 1

I was surprised that temporary sexual-identity confusion was not mentioned in the literature as a commonly occurring symptom because all six of my analysands had at one time or another worried about their sexual identity. But these worries were not deep-seated developmental lags or consequences of preverbal trauma. They were most often responses to the incest that made my analysands confused. Because they had to hide from themselves the fact that the most important figures in their lives had wronged them, they also had to hide loving and hating their parents in order to ensure continued psychological growth. Because of their ambivalent responses to present important others, including me, they appeared at times to be borderline personalities. The crucial difference was that they did not stick to the characterologic vacillations toward objects that have been described by Kernberg (1975, 1976) and others as a stable feature of borderline conditions, nor did they split their internalized objects into all-good and all-bad figures. As my case histories show, their ambivalence was not part and parcel of their parental introject but a response to the incestuous trauma inflicted on them. They both loved and hated their parental abusers; but, in contrast to borderline patients, they were aware of their ambivalence and knew that they were directing it at one and the same person. Developmentally speaking, each of the people I reported on had reached some sort of oedipal configuration, which as is well known, is an important factor because the presence of inner structure, no matter how distorted, makes an analysis, including reconstructions, possible.

The symptoms every one of my incestuously abused analysands showed were (1) lack of trust in interpersonal relationships; (2) temporary sexual identity confusion; (3) motoric discharge patterns. This triad also suggests the borderline category (Kernberg, 1975, 1976). Despite my patients' faulty reality testing, however, I did not find the lack of differentiation between self and object, the inability to experience present objects as other than a replay of past ones, and the vulnerability to transference interpretation that Kernberg assigns to borderline personalities. Although at times there were pronounced contradictory swings in mood and transference manifestations, these swings were not as primitive as those Kernberg (1976) describes (pp. 162–163). Because the trauma occurred much later than that of borderline patients, the fear of fragmentation and splitting was not as pervasive. The nonverbal aspects, motoric discharge, and expression of conflict were a reaction of speechlessness and shock to the abuse, not fixations in the preverbal area. It is possible, therefore, that these abused patients were analyzable.

The three symptomatic features just mentioned could also be seen as manifestations of narcissistic personality disorders. Kohut (1971) postulates a split-off, idealized parent imago for the narcissistic personality. This idealized imago cannot be transmuted by experience but stays fixed in relationship to the narcissistic, grandiose self, which is also split off and disavowed (p. 83). But my analysands were quickly able, within the transference, to transcend their distrust and habitual caution toward important others without exhibiting narcissistic vulnerability. When their narcissistic defenses dissolved, I was not in the presence of an unstructured psyche but was confronted with people who were struggling valiantly to understand their oedipal drama, including the incestuous parent. Nevertheless, I on occasion proceeded to ascribe a narcissistic personality disorder to one or another of these analysands. Their transferences often consisted of an open idealization of their analyst. But when the analysands became aware of their unrealistic expectations toward me, they did not collapse in rageful vulnerability. Instead, they were able to mourn the childhood and the good-enough parents they might have had. This mourning would not have been possible if they had already been traumatized during infancy, when internal structuring had not yet taken place.

It can be seen that at this point in our knowledge we cannot make a priori judgments about who was incestuously abused and who was not, whether we are dealing with people who have deeply repressed the memory or those who appear before us ready with the accusation of incest. (An exception would be those who are still entangled in incestuous acts.)

In view of all the factors cited, I submit that we cannot and should not attempt to create a separate diagnostic category for victims of incest. I have fantasized about creating a questionnaire to be sent to all analysts, asking them if they have treated people with incestuous trauma in their backgrounds and what symptoms and adaptations they found. Then perhaps we could gather the data necessary to make a sweeping generalization constituting a diagnosis.

REVEALING COUNTERTRANSFERENCE

While writing this book I have often referred to the importance of countertransference. I described what I felt in some
detail but did not reflect on why my countertransference
became my most reliable guide in sorting out whether or not
the patient had experienced overt incest. The information I
gathered from examining my countertransference did inform
my interpretations, although I never directly said to a patient:
"Yes, you were abused," or "No, you weren't." The process of
analyzing brought the patients close enough to their realities
for them either to confirm or to dismiss their own suspicions.
While they seldom commented about how they perceived me,
I became convinced that they were influenced by my feeling
states. An intersubjective space arose that permitted intimacy
without intrusion for both partners in the analytic dyad. This
subtle exchange of feelings, when not overshadowed by transference constellations, was close to a good working alliance. I
could often hear an echo of my particular moods in my
analysands' affective coloration either during the reports of
memory or during associating. But because I did not concret-
ize my analysands' experience by confirming it, they felt free
to investigate by themselves what had befallen them. Emotional
acceptance of another's world of emotions is not the same as
sharing beliefs. For instance, I could resonate with the fear of
abandonment that Ms. Waugh brought to her sessions. But this
did not mean that in fantasy I aided her in pursuing Terry.
Corroborating Mrs. Raphael's and Mrs. Hutchinson's traumas
outside the analysis might also be seen as distrustful within the
transference. Yet, it is my impression that they felt keenly that
I was emotionally with them most of the time and therefore
they were able to bear up under what I came to see as my
counterresistance to becoming directly involved in their search
for certainty. I believed the evidence uncovered during analytic sessions was proof enough. I found that I was unable to
fine tune my countertransference to their realistic detective
work. Perhaps this had to do with my idealizing of psychoanalysis as a treatment.

COUNTERTRANSFERENCE ENACTMENT

In the early chapters, I delineated my struggles to free myself
from disbelief and distortions. In perusing what I have said

about my feelings while treating incest victims, it can be seen that I never lost my horror of incest and resisted its full impact on my analytic sensibility. When I "knew" that a patient was about to reveal incestuous trauma, I was often perturbed and unwilling to let the flow of sympathy, anger, personal recollections, and reawakened conflict wash over me. But my fear of these reactivations of my own inner struggles gradually subsided. I accepted them as part of my treatment repertoire. I learned to differentiate my somatic responses to analysands' material according to what they brought into the treatment. This was true for all the people I treated. Distinctive echoes of each patient's psychological fate lodged themselves in me. The strength of these echoes was not always the result of the patient's needs but of my own. I noted that vigilance was needed in the self-analytic process. Some "merely" neurotic patients could be as difficult to accompany countertransferentially as borderline or narcissistic ones were, if their conflicts reactivated mine. I found Racker's (1953) concept of a countertransference neurosis helpful. It made sense to me that experiencing and solving conflicts within the countertransference enables the analyst to live first-hand, not second-hand, what is going on with the patient. Such an undertaking is precarious because it presupposes a readiness on the part of the analyst to become temporarily neurotic herself. Bollas (1983) describes it well:

> We know that the analytic space and process facilitates regressive elements in the analyst as well as in the patient, so each analyst working with, rather than against, the countertransference must be prepared, on occasion, to become rather situationally ill, in so far as his receptivity to the reliving of the patient's transference will inevitably mean that the patient's representation of disturbed bits of the mother, or the father, or elements of the infant self, will be utilized in the transference usage of the analyst [pp. 5–6].

It must be underscored that Bollas does not advocate spilling the countertransference neurosis into the sessions. Yet this can easily occur when involvement is deep and lasting. For instance, my spontaneous laughter at experiencing borborygmi in tandem with Mr. Brewster, or the supportive comments made to Ms. Laviza could be seen as unduly close. But these are benign examples that propelled the treatment, not necessarily altogether psychoanalytic in nature, forward. These responses were still more or less connected to my work ego and useful to the patients. There were other instances that were not so benign yet taught me how important it is to be aware of the regressive pull arising out of a patient's transference. I must add that, for me, it was not always the most deeply impaired patients who pulled me into their orbit. Certainly the people I describe in this book were not the most deeply regressed I have worked with, yet listening to them produced a wish in me to rescue them immediately, more for my sake than for theirs. In the attempt to analyze their victimization, I sometimes formed a clearer picture of their important others than of them. It was as though I could not abide negative character traits or hostility in these particular analysands. I wanted to see them as purified by suffering, an idealizing stance hardly conducive to in-depth work. I eventually realized that each of these treatments brought me in touch with the fantasy of being, or becoming, the world's best analyst, who never had to resort to parameters and always found the right interpretation delivered with unfailing tact and timing.

Fortunately for my analysands, I had a wide variety of patients when one or another of my incestuously misused patients unwittingly stirred grandiose fantasies in me. Because of a countertransference enactment in regard to a woman afflicted by a narcissistic personality disorder, I understood that this grandiose wish was a defense against my relative helplessness in certain treatment impasses. The lady, Mrs. Corcoran, considered herself a perfect patient, yet all interpretation slithered off without even being heard. I often felt like telling her that I could no longer work with her, that she was not analyzable, at least not by me. But she seemed to register my unspoken despair and to forestall my intent by producing a dream or a bit of insight just when I thought I could no longer tolerate her smug self-righteousness. She was in the habit of extolling my virtues and those of psychoanalysts in general, claiming us to be the chosen, superior mutation who would save the world from perdition. At the same time, she held political views opposite from mine; she derided liberal views as the product of uninformed, uncouth, eternally fornicating, racially mongrelized extremists. While I understood these speeches to be defenses against great vulnerability, I also felt enormous anger and an unwillingness to lend my analytic self to her.

Because I felt guilty about such thoughts, I agreed to a change of time for her sessions that was most inconvenient for me. I arrived breathlessly but punctually in my office only to find that she did not appear. She did appear at the old time, though, and became enraged when she saw that it had been given to someone else. When we met again, she claimed that I had locked both the front and the back doors of the building so that she could not come in. After waiting for me for half an hour she went home, she declared. I knew this declaration to be false because the next patient had walked in without difficulty. But instead of trying to understand where her delusional accusation came from, I confronted her with the realities. She appeared to understand. Not so. She brought the incident up over and over again, seemingly searching for confirmation from me that I, not she, was delusional. I sought consultation and was told that the patient had tried to induce in me what she felt. The trouble with that advice was that I do not believe a patient can induce any feeling that the analyst has not already experienced through her own perceptual apparatus. While I was mulling over whether my belief was grandiose, it occurred to me that this attitude might not only be grandiose but also delusional in nature. Obviously, no one can incorporate all feeling states of everyone at once. If this attitude was what I had used to fend off Mrs. Corcoran, she was right in trying to persuade me to accept delusion as part of my psyche. Much humbled, I waited for the next barrage of accusations and used it to acknowledge that I might have misread her intent. The reality of the situation became entirely unimportant at once. Mrs. Corcoran was able to say what she really meant: she felt neglected and misunderstood by me. She had not needed a change of hours but had requested it to test me. She had not come at the new hour because she hoped I would understand her request as a way of saying how locked out she felt. We still had a rocky road to hew after that, but my negative countertransference dropped away as I began to understand Mrs. Corcoran's obliquely stated needs.

Keeping a notebook about what I felt about each patient helped enormously in formulating predictive and interpretive hypotheses. The later entries are not nearly so detailed as the earlier ones. For me, it was not the developmental level of any given analysand that produced strong or difficult countertransference. Rather, I reacted according to the ability of the patient to reactivate my own conflicts. When I finally was able to let go of some grandiose fantasies of my own—such as attempting to be an unfailingly empathic and correct analyst—I found the inner freedom to accept my shortcomings. I also began to understand the roots of some of my theoretical assumptions. For instance, I am aware that it has become standard technique for a number of analysts to reveal their countertransference, especially in work with patients who suffer from preoedipal disorders (Epstein and Feiner, 1979; Gorkin, 1987). While the theoretical formulations about countertransferential revelations make a good deal of sense to me, I have no enthusiasm for them. Because I include nonverbal aspects of the analysands' communication in my interpretations, I obviously reveal how closely I observe. Analysands frequently appear to be gratified by my attention although I always preface my interpretation of nonverbal aspects by saying, "It appears that . . ." or "could it be that . . . ." These phrases alert the patient to the fact that disagreement with my perceptions is not dangerous, that he or she has the last word. I cannot recollect allowing myself to verbalize what I felt during long silences or directly accusing a patient of wishing to murder me notwithstanding that I was quite certain at times that such intent existed.

Bion (1955) recounts interpreting the murderous rage he felt in the atmosphere created nonverbally by a schizoid patient. I admire his courage in doing so but would not use the same technique myself. Following a supervisor's suggestion, I tried to interpret similar feelings and nonverbal communications created by schizoid patients. I found that instead of my becoming more attuned to their behavior, my intervention confirmed for them that they were indeed murderers. They did not feel relief on being told what I perceived but felt that they were in fact murderers. In general, I found that I achieved better understanding of a patient's nonverbal behavior if I waited to see if he or she would verbalize it. I found it hard to tolerate their long silences but discovered that these silences were also communications to me, meaning that the patients were not ready to admit their hostility or pain or confusion. Later, many of them told me that they had become afraid of my "penetrating eyes like x-rays" anyway. They apparently transferred their own omnipotence to me and then felt totally bereft of all power when I tried to speak of what I felt in their silences.

I am by now also aware that despite my well-reasoned theoretical convictions about not revealing countertransference, I am in part influenced by an experience I had early in my own analysis. When my analyst prepared for his summer break I was sad to see him go but also glad that I would have more time to pursue interests I had no time for in a demanding schedule. I withheld this piece of information but made up my mind to tell him about it when he returned. I also felt very clever in discovering during the summer break, that my not being as open as usual constituted a holding on to him while he was gone. During the first session following his vacation, I told him how glad I was to see him and how glad I had been to have extra time. He at first said nothing but at the end of the hour told me that he had thought of me during the break. I was devastated by this piece of news. It felt to me as though from then on I would have to be very careful about what I told him so as not to burden him. Fortunately he already knew enough about my background to notice my changed transference and interpret my reluctance. My mother had felt intensely burdened by me, and I replayed my protective attitude toward her with my analyst. Not a surprising state of affairs but one that deeply influenced me not to be forthcoming with countertransference statements.

When I eventually decided to become an analyst myself, I learned about the havoc a mother transference can produce and quickly linked this information with the foregoing episode. I was still in analysis then and had an opportunity once more to hash through the whole incident. I learned that my mother had provided good training for an analyst. Her unspoken needs had taught me how to read other people's feelings without letting on that I could do so. Nonetheless, there were times when I admitted to feeling states related to my patients' material when such disclosure was in the service of reality testing by vulnerable persons. I have described in detail how I responded to borborigmy during the treatment of Val Brewster. There, my unanalytic spontaneity actually helped the course of the analysis. But the analysis remained incomplete. Mr. Brewster could not tolerate mourning caused by entry into the individuation process. Possibly my response was involved in concretizing this inability.

SPECIFIC USE OF COUNTERTRANSFERENCE

When working with incest victims, I seemed to know that they had been abused before they realized it themselves. I mistrusted these perceptions because they appeared to be a tuning in to preconscious processes of remembering. I did not relish the role of Cassandra, even though I did not make public my suspicions. At times, I adopted a superior, oh-not-again stance in order to defend myself. But this did not mean that I was unavailable to the patient. On the contrary, this seeming arrogance was a mirror of the patients' struggle to integrate the inexplicable by making believe that it was commonplace to have been incestuously used. On the other hand, I defended against feeling fully with the patient and focused on how I felt about the parental introject. This maneuver often helped me to overcome unpleasant somatic responses until I could get a more complete picture of the patient's internal perceptions. In particular, the experience of mutual borborigmy brought me a step closer to demystifying my own responses and accepting physiologic responsiveness as part and parcel of my work ego. Once I had begun to differentiate which response I brought to which situation, both countertransference and my resistance to it became useful tools. At first, I was shocked at the hostility that surfaced on occasion and censored myself. But I soon noted that not accepting hostility as a valid response made my interpretive work a rather boring intellectual task during which I had to laboriously gather details. The same task became a smooth interactive field once I allowed myself to be imperfect. This imperfection included acknowledging that psychoanalysis is not only a science but also an art that recreates itself according to the need at hand. Thus, while many of my patients learned to stop idealizing their important others, I learned to stop idealizing psychoanalysis.

References

Abend, S. M. (1989), Countertransference and psychoanalytic technique. *Psychoanal. Quart.*, 58:374–395.

Anthi, P. R. (1983), Reconstruction of preverbal experiences. *J. Amer. Psychoanal. Assn.*, 31:33–58.

Bernstein, A. (1989), Analysis of two adult females who had been victims of incest in childhood. *J. Amer. Acad. Psychoanal.*, 17:207–221.

—— (1990), The impact of incest trauma on ego development. In: *Adult Analysis and Childhood Sexual Abuse,* ed. H. Levine. Hillsdale, NJ: The Analytic Press, pp. 65–91.

Berry, G. W. (1975), Incest: Some clinical variations on a clinical theme. *J. Amer. Acad. Psychoanal.*, 3:151–161.

Bion, W. R. (1955), Language and the Schizophrenic. In: *New Directions in Psychoanalysis,* ed. M. Klein, P. Heiman & R. E. Money-Kyrle. London: Tavistock, pp. 220–234.

—— (1963), *Elements of Psychoanalysis.* London: Heinemann.

Blum, H. (1977), The prototype of preoedipal reconstruction. *J. Amer. Psychoanal. Assn.*, 25:757–786.

Bollas, C. (1983), Expressive uses of countertransference. *Contemp. Psychoanal.*, 19:1–34.

Brenner, C. (1971), The psychoanalytic concept of aggression. *Internat. J. Psycho-Anal.*, 52:137–144.

Cohler, B. J. (1987), Sex, love and incest. *Contemp. Psychoanal.*, 19:1–34.

Da Silva, G.(1990), Borborygmi as markers of psychic work during analytic sessions. *Internat. J. Psycho-Anal.*, 71:641–660.

Davies, J. M. & Frawley, M. G. (1992), Dissociative processes and transference–countertransference paradigms in the psychoanalytic oriented treatment of adult survivors of childhood sexual abuse. *Psychoanal. Dial.*, 1:5–36.

Deutsch, F. (1955), *The Clinical Interview.* New York: International Universities Press.

Deutsch, H. (1942), Some forms of emotional disturbance and their relationship to schizophrenia. *Psychoanal. Quart.*, 11:301–321.

Devore, I. & Konnor, M. J. (1974), Infancy in hunter-gatherer life: An ethological perspective. In: *Ethology and Psychiatry,* ed. N. White. Toronto: University of Toronto Press, pp. 39–50.

Dewald, P. (1989), Effects on an adult of incest in childhood A case report. *J. Amer. Psychoanal. Assn.,* 37:997–1014.

Diamond, D. (1989), Father–daughter incest; Unconscious fantasy and social fact. *Psychoanal. Psychol.,* 6:421–437.

Dickes, R. (1965), The defensive functions of an altered state of consciousness. *J. Amer. Psychoanal. Assn.,* 13:356–403.

Dorpat, T. (1988), Foreword. In: *Female Homosexuality* by E. V. Siegel. Hillsdale, NJ: The Analytic Press, pp. xiii–xxii.

—— (1983), The cognitive arrest hypothesis of denial. *Internat. J. Psycho-Anal.,* 64:47–58.

Ehrenberg, D. B. (1987), Abuse and desire: A case of father–daughter incest. *Contemp. Psychoanal.,* 23:593–604.

Epstein, L. Feiner, A. H. (1979), *Countertransference.* New York: Aronson.

Ferenczi, S. (1930), The principle of relaxation and neocatharsis. In: *Final Contributions to the Problems and Methods of Psychoanalysis.* London: Hogarth Press, 1955, pp. 108–125.

—— (1949), Confusion of tongues between adults and the child: The language of tenderness and the language of passion. *Internat. J. Psycho-Anal.,* 30:225–230.

Finkelhor, D. (1979), *Sexually Victimized Children.* New York: Free Press.

Fliess, R. (1953), The hypnotic evasion of an altered state of consciousness. *Psychoanal. Quart.,* 22:497–511.

Frank, A. (1969), The unrememberable and the unforgettable: Passive primal repression. *The Psychoanalytic Study of the Child,* 24:44–77. New York: International Universities Press.

Freud, S. (1895), Project for a scientific psychology. *Standard Edition,* 1:283–397. London: Hogarth Press, 1966.

—— (1986), The aetiology of hysteria. *Standard Edition,* 3:189–221. London: Hogarth Press, 1962.

—— (1905), Three essays on the theory of sexuality. *Standard Edition,* 7:125–243. London: Hogarth Press, (1953).

—— (1914), On the history of the psychoanalytic movement. *Standard Edition,* 14:7–66. London: Hogarth Press, 1963.

—— (1915), Observations on transference love. *Standard Edition,* 12:157–171. London: Hogarth Press, 1958.

—— (1916), Some character types met with in psychoanalytic work. *Standard Edition,* 14:309–322. London: Hogarth Press, 1957.

—— (1917), Introductory lectures on psycho-analysis. *Standard Edition,* 17:7–123. London: Hogarth Press, 1955.

—— (1925), Negation. *Standard Edition,* 19:235–239. London: Hogarth Press, 1961.

—— (1932), New introductory lectures on psychoanalysis. *Standard Edition,* 22:1–182. London: Hogarth Press, 1964.

Furman, A. & Furman, E. (1984), Intermittent decathexis—a type of parental dysfunction. *Internat. J. Psycho-Anal.,* 65:423–234.

Furst, S. (1967), *Psychic Trauma.* New York: Basic Books.

Gabbard, G. O. & Twemlow, S. W. (1994), Mother–son incest in the pathogenesis of narcissistic personality organization. *J. Amer. Psychoanal. Assn.,* 42:171–190.

Goodwin, J. U., McCarthy, T. & DiVasto, P. (1981), Prior incest in abusive mothers. *Child Abuse & Neglect,* 5:1–9.

Gorkin, M. (1987), *The Uses of Countertransference.* Northvale, NJ: Aronson.

Greenacre, P. (1941), *Trauma, Growth and Personality.* New York: International Universities Press, pp. 7–52, 1969.

—— (1971), The influence of infantile trauma on genetic patterns. In: *Emotional Growth, Vol. 1,* New York: International Universities Press, pp. 260–299.

—— (1975), On reconstruction. J. Amer. Psychoanal. Assn. 23:693–713.

Greenson, R. (1968), *The Technique and Practice of Psychoanalysis, Vol. 1.* New York: International Universities Press.

Herman, L., Russel, D. & Trackl, K. (1986), Long-term effects of incestuous abuse in childhood. *Amer. J. Psychiat.,* 143:1293–1296.

—— & Schatzow, E. (1987), Recovery and verification of childhood sexual trauma. *Psychoanal. Psychol.,* 4:1–14.

Holland, N. H. (1989), Masonic wrongs. *Amer. Imago,* 46:329–352.

Huizenga, J. (1990), Incest as trauma: A Psychoanalytic case. In: *Adult Analysis and Childhood Sexual Abuse,* ed. H. Levine. Hillsdale, NJ: The Analytic Press, pp. 117–135.

Irving, B. (1964), Survey on incest. *Excerpt. Criminol.,* 4:137–155.

Jacobs, T. J. (1973), Posture, gesture and movement in the analyst: Cues to interpretation and countertransference. *J. Amer. Assn.,* 21:77–92.

—— (1986), On countertransference enactment. *J. Amer. Psychoanal. Assn.,* 34:289–308.

Jaffe, D. S. (1986), Empathy, counteridentification, countertransference: A review with some personal perspectives on the "analytic instrument." *Psychoanal. Quart.,* 55:215–243.

Katan, A. (1973), Children who were raped. *The Psychoanalytic Study of the Child,* 28:208–224. New Haven, CT: Yale University Press.

Kernberg, O. (1975), *Borderline Conditions and Pathologic Narcissism.* New York: Aronson.

—— (1976), *Object Relations Theory and Clinical Psychoanalysis.* New York: Aronson.

Kestenberg, J. (1967), *The Role of Movement Patterns in Development.* New York: Dance Notation Bureau, 1974.

King, K. R. & Dorpat, T. L., (1992), Daddy's girl: An interactional perspective on the transference of defense in the psychoanalysis of a case of father–daughter incest. In: *Psychoanalytic Perspectives on Women,* ed. E. V. Siegel. New York: Brunner Mazel, pp. 63–88.

Kohut, H. (1959), Introspection, empathy and psychoanalysis. An examination of the relationship between mode of observation and theory. *J. Amer. Psychoanal., Assn.,* 7:459–483.

—— (1971), *The Analysis of the Self.* New York: International Universities Press.

—— (1977), *The Restoration of the Self.* New York: International Universities Press.

Kramer, S., (1983), Object-coercive doubting: A pathologic defensive response to maternal incest. *J. Amer. Psychoanal. Assn.,* 31:325–351.

—— (1990), Residues of incest. In: *Adult Analysis and Childhood Sexual Abuse.,* ed. H. Levine. Hillsdale, NJ: The Analytic Press, pp. 149–170.

—— & Akhtar, S. (1991), *The Trauma of Transgression:* Northvale, NJ: Aronson.

Kris, E. (1956), The personal myth: A problem in psychoanalytic technique. *J. Amer. Psychoanal. Assn.,* 4:653–681.

Krystal, H. (1978), Trauma and affects. *The Psychoanalytic Study of the Child.* 33:81–116. New Haven, CT: Yale University Press.

Laban, R. (1969), *The Mastery of Movement.* London: MacDonald & Evans.

Laufer, M. (1994), Sexual abuse, or a delusional structure? From adolescent to Young adult. *The Psychoanalytic Study of the Child,* 49:208–221. New Haven, CT: Yale University Press.

Levine, H., ed. (1990a), *Adult Analysis and Childhood Sexual Abuse.* Hillsdale, NJ: The Analytic Press.

—— (1990b), Clinical issues in the analysis of adults who were sexually abused as children. In: *Adult and Childhood Sexual Abuse,* ed. H. Levine. Hillsdale, NJ: The Analytic Press, pp. 197–218.

Levy, S. T. & Inderbitzin, L. B. (1992), Neutrality, interpretation, and therapeutic intent. *J. Amer. Psychoanal. Assn.,* 40:989–1012.

Lichtenberg, J. (1983), *Psychoanalysis and Infant Research.* Hillsdale, NJ: The Analytic Press.

Lipton, S. (1977), The advantages of Freud's technique as shown in his analysis of the Rat Man. *Internat. J. Psycho- Anal.* 58:255-274.

Lisman-Piesczanski, N. (1990), Countertransference in the analysis of an adult who was sexually abused as a child. In: *Adult Analysis of Childhood Sexual Abuse,* ed. H. Levine, Hillsdale, NJ: The Analytic Press, pp. 138-147.

Little, M. (1951), Countertransference and the patient's response to it. *Internat. J. Psycho-Anal.,* 32:32-40.

Mahler, M. (1968), *On Human Symbiosis and the Vicissitudes of Individuation.* New York: International Universities Press.

—— (1971), A study of the separation-individuation process and its possible application to borderline phenomena in the psychoanalytic situation. *The Psychoanalytic Study of the Child,* 26:403-424. New Haven, CT: Yale University Press.

—— Pine, F. & Bergman, A. (1975), *The Psychological Birth of the Human Infant.* New York: Basic Books.

Marcus, B. F. (1989), Incest and the borderline syndrome; The mediating role of identity. *Psychoanal. Psychol.,* 6:199-217.

Margolis, M. (1977), A preliminary report of a case of consummated mother–son incest. *The Annual of Psychoanalysis,* 5:267-293. New York: International Universities Press.

—— (1984), A case of mother–adolescent son incest: A follow-up study. *Psychoanal. Quart.,* 53:355-385.

Masson, J. M. (1984), *The Assault on Truth.* New York: Farrar, Strauss, Giroux.

—— ed. (1985), *The Complete Letters of Sigmund Freud to Wilhelm Fliess, 1987-1904.* Cambridge, MA: Harvard University Press.

McDougall, J. (1989), *Theatres of the Body.* London: Free Association Books.

McLaughlin, J. T. (1992), Nonverbal behaviors in the analytic situation: The search for meaning in nonverbal cues. In: *When the Body Speaks,* ed. S. Kramer & S. Akhtar. Northvale, NJ: Aronson, pp. 132-161.

Mittelman, B. (1957), Motility in infants, children and adults; Patterning and psychodynamics. *The Psychoanalytic Study of the Child,* 9:142-177. New York: International Universities Press.

—— (1955), Motor patterns in genital behavior: Fetishism. *The Psychoanalytic Study of the Child,* 10:241-263. New York: International Universities Press.

—— (1957) Motility in the therapy of children and adults. *The Psychoanalytic Study of the Child,* 12:284-319. New York: International Universities Press.

Mrazek, P. B. & Kempe, C. H. (1981), *Sexually Abused Children and Their Families.* New York: Pergamon Press.

Nachmani, G. (1987), Fathers who mistake their daughters for their mothers. *Contemp. Psychoanal.*, 23:621–630.

Panel (1977), Nonverbal aspects of child and adult psychoanalysis (R. Lilleskov, reporter). *J. Amer. Psychoanal. Assn.*, 25:679–692.

Panel (1988), The seduction hypothesis (A. E. Marans, reporter). *J. Amer. Psychoanal. Assn.*, 36:759–772.

Racker, H. (1953), A contribution to the problem of countertransference. *Internat. J. Psycho-Anal.*, 34:331–324.

—— (1955), The meanings and uses of countertransference. *Psychoanal. Quart.*, 25:303–357.

Raphling, D. (1990), Technical issues of the opening phase. In: *Adult Analysis of Childhood Sexual Abuse*, ed. H. Levine. Hillsdale, NJ: The Analytic Press, pp. 45–64.

—— (1994), A patient who was not sexually abused. *J. Amer. Psychoanal. Assn.*, 42:65–77.

Rascovsky, A. & Rascovsky, M. (1972), The prohibition of incest, filicide and the sociocultural process. *Internat. J. Psycho-Anal.*, 53:271–276.

Roiphe, H. & Galenson, E. (1981), *Infantile Origins of Sexual Identity*. New York: International Universities Press.

Sandler, J. & Joffe, W. G. (1967), The tendency to persistence in psychological function and development. *Bull. Menninger Clin.*, 31:257–272.

Schilder, P. (1950), *The Image and Appearance of the Human Body*. New York: International Universities Press.

Schur, M. (1955), Comments on the metapsychology of somatization. *The Psychoanalytic Study of the Child*, 10:119–164. New York: International Universities Press.

Shengold, L. (1963), The parent as sphinx. *J. Amer. Psychoanal. Assn.*, 11:725–751.

—— (1980), Some reflections on a case of mother–adolescent son incest. *Internat. J. Psycho-Anal.*, 61:461–475.

—— (1989), *Soul Murder*. New Haven, Ct.: Yale University Press.

—— (1991), A variety of narcissistic pathology stemming from parental weakness. *Psychoanal. Quart.*, 60:86–92.

Sherkow, S. P. (1990a), Evaluation and diagnosis of sexual abuse of little girls. *J. Amer. Psychoanal. Assn.*, 38:347–370.

—— (1990b), Consequences of childhood sexual abuse on the development of ego structure: A comparison of child and adult cases. In: *Adult Analysis and Childhood Sexual Abuse*, ed. H. Levine. Hillsdale, NJ: The Analytic Press, pp. 93–116.

Siegel, E. V. (1984), *Dance Therapy: The Mirror of Our Selves*. New York: Human Sciences Press.

—— (1988), *Female Homosexuality*. Hillsdale, NJ: The Analytic Press.

—— (1991), *Middle-Class Waifs*. Hillsdale, NJ: The Analytic Press.

—— (1994), Clinical observations of the sexual and sensual transference in women. *Psychoanal. Inq.*, 14:591–603.

—— Trautmann-Voigt, S. & Voigt, B. (1996), *Analytische Bewegungstlerapic: Theorie und Praxis*. Frankfurt, Main: Fischer Taschenbuch Verlag.

Silber, A. (1979), Childhood seduction, parental pathology and hysterical symptomatology: The genesis of altered states of consciousness. *Internat. J. Psycho-Anal.*, 60:109–116.

Simon, B. (1992), Incest—see under Oedipus complex: The history of an error in psychoanalysis. *J. Amer. Psychoanal. Assn.*, 40:955–988.

Soll, M. H. (1984–1985), The transferable penis and the self-representation. *Internat. J. Psycho-Anal. Psychother.*, 10:473–493.

Spruiell, V. (1986), Trying to understand the consequences or lack of consequences of overt sexuality between adults and children. Panel presentation, American Psychoanalytic Association, Dec. 21.

Stern, D. (1985), *The Interpersonal World of the Infant*. New York: Basic Books.

Stoller, R. J. (1977), Primary femininity. In: *Female Psychology*, ed. H. P. Blum. New York: International Universities Press, pp. 59–78.

—— (1985), *Presentations of Gender*. New Haven, CT: Yale University Press.

Stolorow, R. D. & Lachmann, F. M. (1980), *Psychoanalysis and Developmental Arrest*. New York: International Press.

Strachey, J. (1934), The nature of the therapeutic action of psychoanalysis. *Internat. J. Psycho-Anal.*, 15:127–159.

Tolpin, M. (1980), Discussion of "Psychoanalytic Theories of the Self: An integration," by M. Shane & E. Shane. In: *Advances in Self Psychology*, ed. A. Goldberg. New York: International Universities Press, pp. 47–68.

Valenstein, A. (1962), Affects, emotional reliving and insight in the psychoanalytic process. *Internat. J. Psycho-Anal.*, 43:315–324.

—— (1989), Pre-oedipal reconstructions in psychoanalysis. *Internat. J. Psycho-Anal.*, 70:433–442.

Weil, J. L. (1989), *Instinctual Stimulation of Children, Vols. 1 & 2*. Madison, CT: International Universities Press.

Weinshel, E. (1986), Perceptual distortions during analysis: Some observations on the role of the superego in reality testing. In: *Psychoanalysis: The Science of Mental Conflicts*. ed. A. Richards & M. Willick. Hillsdale, NJ: The Analytic Press.

Welles, J. K. & Wrye, H. K. (1991), Maternal erotic transference. *Internat. J. Psycho-anal.* 72:93–106.

Westen, D., Ludoph, P., Misle, B., Ruffins, S. & Block, J. (1990), Physical and sexual abuse in adolescent girls with borderline personality. *Amer. J. Orthopsychiat.*, 60:55–66.

Wolf, E. K. & Alpert, J. L. (1991), Psychoanalysis and childhood sexual abuse: A review of the literature. *Psychoanal. Psychol.*, 8:305–328.

Woodbury J. & Schwartz, E. (1971) *The Silent Sin.* New York: Signet Books.

Index

Index